Rock Solid Faith

Book Three

By Dr. Micheal Spencer

TABLE OF CONTENTS

INTRODUCTION (PAGE 3)

CHAPTER 1: WATER BAPTISM (PAGE 4)

CHAPTER 2: SPIRITUAL BAPTISM (PAGE 10)

CHAPTER 3: LAYING ON OF HANDS (PAGE 20)

CHAPTER 4: THE RAPTURE OF THE CHURCH AND THE RESURRECTIONS (PAGE 32)

BIBLICAL TIMELINE (PAGE 44)

CHAPTER 5: JUDGEMENTS (PAGE 45)

CHAPTER 6: TITHE - SEED – ALMS (PAGE 53)

2 Timothy 2:15

Be diligent to present yourself approved to God, a worker who does not need to be ashamed, rightly dividing the word of truth. NKJV

The body of Christ loves the Lord, yet so many in the body do not know who they are, what they are, or what they believe. Ignorance has saturated the saints of Christ. We can shout, we can dance, but the majority of Christians cannot give a reason for why they believe the Bible is true.

The passion of this text is to empower the sons and daughters of faith through knowledge of the Word of God, so that when all the shaking is done, they are still standing. I challenge you to read, study, and then re-digest this book over and over again so that you will KNOW who you are in Jesus, and what your purpose is on this planet.

Thank you for investing in your spirit man! Your investment will bring stability to your spirit, soul, and body, and you will reap a HUGE harvest in your everyday walk with Jesus.

Get ready! Pull out your napkin and utensils, it's time to EAT!

I would like to thank some people who helped to make this happen. My loving wife Rhonda, and my family have sacrificed many hours of my time so this could be penned. I would also like to thank Dr. Keith Johnson for pushing and encouraging me to finish this book. A special thank you to Pastor Mary Edlin and Evangelist Ted Shuttlesworth for your years of speaking into my life and teaching me so I could teach others. I would also like to thank Nicole Colwell for editing the text, and MRCCC Publishing for publishing the book. This is not one person's work, but the collection of so many individuals who made Volume 3 of **TRUTH: Rock Solid Faith** come to fruition.

With sincere love,

Dr. Micheal J. Spencer

Chapter 1

Water Baptism

Hebrews 6:1-2
Therefore, leaving the discussion of the elementary principles of Christ, let us go on to perfection, not laying again the foundation of repentance from dead works and of faith toward God, ²of the doctrine of baptisms, of laying on of hands, of resurrection of the dead, and of eternal judgment. NKJV

I. ...of the doctrine of baptisms

A. As we look at this text, we can tell that there is not just ONE baptism. The word is plural, so we are going to look at the multiple baptisms and bring an understanding to this part of the principles for our spiritual foundation.

B. The two baptisms we will cover are:

1. Baptism in water.

2. Baptism in the Holy Spirit, with the evidence of speaking in tongues.

II. Baptism in Water

A. Misconceptions

1. As previously discussed, some denominations believe that when you are baptized as a baby, you are now going to heaven.

a. Baby baptism has no Biblical precedence and has no eternal value.

b. Baby baptism gets the child wet and mad. It is good religion, but not good Bible.

2. There are denominations that teach that if you are not baptized "in the name of Jesus," you cannot go to heaven.

a. They teach that if you are baptized in the name of the "Father, Son, Holy Ghost," it does not count.

3. When I was baptized at a young age, it was explained to me that the purpose is to show on the outside what has happened on the inside. So when you get baptized, it is really just an outward testimony and that is the whole of it.

4. All these ideals are interesting and many not only hold to these principles but would die for these principles. The problem is that they are not based on the Word of God and that is our measuring stick, not religion and denominational decrees.

5. So, if all these ideals are not the Bible's ideals, then what does the Bible say about water baptism?

B. The Word of God Concerning Water Baptism

1. The root word for baptism is the Greek word, "bapto" meaning, "to *whelm*, that is, cover wholly with a fluid" (*Strong's Exhaustive Concordance* G911).

a. Baptized - **G907** *bap-tid'-zo* From a derivative of G911So this verse shows that when John the Baptist baptized Jesus of Nazareth that Jesus was submerged in the water, not sprinkled.; to *make whelmed* (that is, *fully wet*); (*Strong's Exhaustive Concordance* G907).

b. In order to be Biblically baptized, it must be by submersion.

2. "For instance, a spendthrift is said to be submerged in debt. A drunk is said to be submerged in drink. A grief-stricken person is said to be submerged in sorrow. A lad before a cross-examining teacher is said to be submerged in questions. The word is regularly used for a ship that has been wrecked and submerged beneath the waves." (William Barclay, pg 265)

a. This shows that sprinkling is not the Biblical principle to be followed. We also have the example that Jesus showed us when He Himself was baptized.

1) *Mark 1:9-11 It came to pass in those days that Jesus came from Nazareth of Galilee, and was **baptized** by John in the Jordan. [10]And immediately, coming up from the water, He saw the heavens parting and the Spirit descending upon Him like a dove. [11]Then a voice came from heaven, "You are My beloved Son, in whom I am well pleased." NKJV*

2) So this verse shows that when John the Baptist baptized Jesus of Nazareth, Jesus was submerged in the water, not sprinkled.

3. Do I have to be baptized to go to heaven?

a. NO.

b. Water baptism will not get you to heaven.

c. There is only one way to heaven and that is to accept Jesus as your personal Savior.

1) I remember once I was called to visit an elderly woman in a hospital. She was not doing well and was not far from death. She gave me the opportunity to share Jesus with her and she desired to be saved and so she asked Jesus into her life. A few moments later, she said that she needed to be baptized or she would not be able to go to heaven. I explained to her that she only needed to receive salvation and that water baptism was important, but not mandatory to go to heaven. She was relieved and a few days later, went home to be with her Lord.

2) Someone once said to me that if a person was not baptized in water, they could not go to heaven. I said their religious belief was sad since that meant that all people who are in prison for life and accept Jesus as their Savior cannot go to heaven. Only a few prisons actually allow water baptism services. I told them how foolish their religious doctrine was and how it just damned a ton of people in jail. They changed their mindset.

3) Paul was irate with the Jews who came in behind him in Galatia because he taught the simple Gospel of salvation and then the religious came behind him and added a ton of "other" things they needed to do to be saved. This is what Paul said to them in Galatians 1:6-9: *I marvel that you are turning away so soon from Him who called you in the grace of Christ, to a different gospel, [7]which is not another; but there are some who trouble you and want to pervert the gospel of Christ. [8]But even if we, or an angel from heaven, preach any other gospel to you than what we have preached to you, let him be accursed. [9]As we have said before, so now I say again, if anyone preaches any other gospel to you than what you have received, let him be accursed. NKJV*

4) *John 14:6 Jesus said to him, "I am the way, the truth, and the life. No one comes to the Father except through Me. NKJV*

4. What is the purpose of water baptism?

a. The purpose is ALWAYS a supernatural result.

b. Jesus never did anything to create a ritual.

c. Whatever Jesus did and showed us to do always has a supernatural result that you can expect to change your life.

d. Water baptism does nothing for your spirit because your spiritual man is now possessed by the Holy Spirit.

> 1) *1 Corinthians 6:19-20 Or do you not know that your body is the temple of the Holy Spirit who is in you, whom you have from God, and you are not your own? ²⁰For you were bought at a price; therefore glorify God in your body and in your spirit, which are God's. NKJV*

> 2) So the work that happens in baptism is working within your soulish man.

e. What is the soulish man? **Please refer to Rock Solid Faith Book 1, Chapter 5 for the teaching on Spirit, Soul, and Body.**

f. The purpose of water baptism is to break the power of the flesh over our lives. This is a supernatural experience that destroys bondages in the soulish realm of a man or woman.

> 1) Soul ties – these are emotional relationships that are not Godly and bring destruction rather than health.

> 2) Addictions – this is anything that you are not in control of. It could be drugs, alcohol, sex, or even television. Whatever controls you other than Jesus.

> 3) Hurts – emotional wounds from the past that hurt you emotionally (brokenhearted – Luke 4:18).

> 4) The power of sin in our lives.

>> a) *Romans 6:1-7 What shall we say then? Shall we continue in sin that grace may abound? ²Certainly not! How shall we who died to sin live any longer in it? ³Or do you not know that as many of us as were baptized into Christ Jesus were baptized into His death? ⁴Therefore we were buried with Him through baptism into death, that just as Christ was raised from the dead by the glory of the Father, even so we also should **walk in newness of life**. ⁵For if we have been united together in the likeness of His death, certainly we also shall be in the likeness of His resurrection, ⁶knowing this, that **our old man was crucified with Him**, that the body of sin might be done*

away with, that **we should no longer be slaves of sin. ⁷For he who has died has been freed from sin**. *NKJV*

b) When we get baptized things change in our lives.

   i. Our nature changes – when we were not serving Jesus, we had the nature or character of our father, the devil.

   - *Ephesians 2:1-3 And you He made alive, who were dead in trespasses and sins, ²in which* **you once walked** *according to the course of this world,* **according to the prince of the power of the air**, *the spirit who now works in the sons of disobedience, ³among whom also we all once conducted ourselves in the lusts of our flesh, fulfilling the desires of the flesh and of the mind, and were by nature children of wrath, just as the others. NKJV*

   - The nature of an unbeliever is that of his father, the devil. It is not that they are worshipping Satan with understanding, but there are only two to choose from; either we serve Satan, or we serve the King of Kings.

   - The nature of an unbeliever is that of sin. Don't be shocked when a sinner acts like a sinner. That is their nature!

   ii. As Christians, we have a NEW nature.

   - *2 Peter 1:2-4 Grace and peace be multiplied to you in the knowledge of God and of Jesus our Lord, ³as His divine power has given to us all things that pertain to life and godliness, through the knowledge of Him who called us by glory and virtue, ⁴by which have been given to us exceedingly great and precious promises, that through these you may* **be partakers of the divine nature**, *having escaped the* *corruption that is in the world through lust. NKJV*

- Sinners have the nature of their father, just like a Christian has the nature of their Father.

- We are made in the likeness of our Daddy!

- YOU HAVE A NEW NATURE!

- We are not sinners (that is nature), we are Christians who choose to sin. You are a saint.

iii. When you are baptized in water, this is where the supernatural power of God is released. Your soulish man is given NEWNESS of life.

- Newness – 2538, the new state of life in which the Holy Spirit places us so as to produce a new state which is eternal life. (Strong's Exhaustive Concordance)

- You are a brand new person - *2 Corinthians 5:17 Therefore, if anyone is in Christ, he is a new creation; old things have passed away; behold, all things have become new. NKJV*

- The old man is crucified. That means your old nature – that of the prince of the power of the air – is broken. You are now able to live within your new nature, the nature of God.

- We are no longer enslaved to sin. We now have a choice to sin or not to sin.

iv. So the power of baptism is very important in the process of living in victory and breaking things off your life from your soulish man.

5) You deserve to be free! GET WATER BAPTIZED!

Chapter 2

Spiritual Baptism

Hebrews 6:1-2
Therefore, leaving the discussion of the elementary principles of Christ, let us go on to perfection, not laying again the foundation of repentance from dead works and of faith toward God, ²of the doctrine of baptisms, of laying on of hands, of resurrection of the dead, and of eternal judgment. NKJV

I. BAPTISM IN THE HOLY SPIRIT

    A. Many Christians have become ashamed of their heritage.

        1. The Baptism of the Holy Spirit with the evidence of speaking with other tongues is the heritage of the Church.

        2. This is a promise to the Church.

        3. *Matthew 3:11 I indeed baptize you with water unto repentance, but He who is coming after me is mightier than I, whose sandals I am not worthy to carry. He will baptize you with the Holy Spirit and fire. NKJV*

        4. *Mark 16:17 And these signs will follow those who believe: In My name they will cast out demons; they will speak with new tongues; NKJV*

II. A PROMISE FROM THE FATHER

    A. *Acts 1:8 But you shall receive power when the Holy Spirit has come upon you; and you shall be witnesses to Me in Jerusalem, and in all Judea and Samaria, and to the end of the earth." NKJV*

        1. Jesus told His disciples to go to Jerusalem and receive the Promise that John the Baptist had been talking about in Matthew 3:11. Jesus was coming to baptize in the Holy Ghost and with Fire.

        2. Jesus prepared people for the Power at different times in the Word.

            a. *John 4:13-14 Jesus answered and said to her, "Whoever drinks of this water will thirst again, ¹⁴but whoever drinks of the water that I shall give him will never thirst. But the water that I shall give him will become in him a fountain of water springing up into everlasting life." NKJV*

3. You Shall Receive Power!

    a. The purpose for the baptism of the Holy Spirit is POWER.

    b. We need more power to WITNESS.

        1) POWER – DUNAMIS

    c. Supernatural ability.

    d. A dynamo – Generating power.

4. There are denominations out there that claim that the POWER was only to validate the disciples in the first century Church and that we do not need that power today. They claim that all the supernatural power manifested in the first century Church ceased and no longer exists in today's church.

    a. If this is true, that means Jesus has left the church powerless in a time when evil is increasing.

5. The world is not getting better.

    a. *Matthew 24:12 And because lawlessness will abound, the love of many will grow cold. NKJV*

    b. *Matthew 24:37 But as the days of Noah were, so also will the coming of the Son of Man be. NKJV*

    c. *2 Timothy 3:1-5 But know this, that in the last days perilous times will come: ²For men will be lovers of themselves, lovers of money, boasters, proud, blasphemers, disobedient to parents, unthankful, unholy, ³unloving, unforgiving, slanderers, without self-control, brutal, despisers of good, ⁴traitors, headstrong, haughty, lovers of pleasure rather than lovers of God, ⁵having a form of godliness but denying its power. And from such people turn away! NKJV*

6. If there was ever a time when the church needs the power, it is today, for we are in the last days. God would not leave his children powerless because Satan is exercising more power. It would defeat God's whole purpose in having us as His light and His salt if we had no way to show the power of God Himself.

III. THE BAPTISM IS A DIFFERENT EXPERIENCE FROM SALVATION

A. Some denominations teach that the baptism of the Holy Spirit happens at the same time as salvation and that tongues are not part of it at all.

B. They teach that when you accept Jesus as your Savior, you are now filled with the Holy Spirit and do not need to speak with other tongues; that tongues were only for the New Testament church.

C. I want to show you through the Word of God that the baptism of the Holy Spirit and salvation are different experiences for believers.

1. One of the first principles to understand is that the disciples lived in Old Testament times.

2. The New Testament did not actually begin until Jesus died and rose from the dead. So the old covenant did not cease until Jesus rose from the dead. Therefore, Jesus and the disciples lived in Old Testament times under the old covenant.

3. In the Old Testament, the old covenant, the Spirit of God came upon people and did not dwell within people.

a. There is one exception. The Spirit of God came upon and dwelled within those who worked and built the tabernacle.

b. The Spirit of God would come upon the Prophets, the Priests, and the Kings, but did not live within them.

c. Jesus also had the Spirit, living within Him. The Spirit of God came upon Jesus when he was baptized in water in Mark 1:9-11.

4. The disciples experienced the same type of salvation that we have today in John 20:22.

a. *John 20:22 And when He had said this, He breathed on them, and said to them, "Receive the Holy Spirit. NKJV*

b. When Jesus breathed on them, they received the Holy Spirit in the same way we receive Him today. Up to this point, they were still living under the old covenant. With this occurrence, they entered into the new covenant because Jesus died and rose again, and the new covenant had been completed.

1) So the disciples had what we have in that the Holy Spirit dwells inside of us. We are the temple of the Holy Ghost.

5. Jesus then instructed them to go to Jerusalem and receive the Promise of the Father.

a. *Acts 1:4-5 And being assembled together with them, He commanded them not to depart from Jerusalem, but to wait for the Promise of the Father, "which," He said, "you have heard from Me; ⁵for John truly baptized with water, but you shall be baptized with the Holy Spirit not many days from now." NKJV*

b. In 1 Corinthians 15:6, it says that over 500 people saw Jesus face-to-face, yet only 120 obeyed Jesus to go to the upper room.

c. *Acts 2:1-4 When the Day of Pentecost had fully come, they were all with one accord in one place. ²And suddenly there came a sound from heaven, as of a rushing mighty wind, and it filled the whole house where they were sitting. ³Then there appeared to them divided tongues, as of fire, and one sat upon each of them. ⁴And they were all filled with the Holy Spirit and began to speak with other tongues, as the Spirit gave them utterance. NKJV*

> 1) We see the manifestation of the Promise of the Father. The Holy Spirit was poured out and people began to speak in other tongues as initial evidence that they received the outpouring.

> 2) This fulfilled the prophetic unction found in the book of Joel, and then repeated here in the book of Acts.

d. *Acts 2:17-19 'And it shall come to pass in the last days, says God, That I will pour out of My Spirit on all flesh; Your sons and your daughters shall prophesy, Your young men shall see visions, Your old men shall dream dreams.¹⁸And on My menservants and on My maidservants I will pour out My Spirit in those days; And they shall prophesy. ¹⁹I will show wonders in heaven above And signs in the earth beneath: NKJV*

> 1) This is the promise that Jesus gave to those who will believe, and it shows a separate experience from that of salvation.

> 2) Even those denominations who do not believe in speaking in other tongues have to agree that this was the evidence that was manifested on the day of Pentecost. Their declaration is that it is no longer for today, not that it did not happen.

> 3) My question is, when did it change? Show me the verse in the Bible where the initial evidence of speaking with other tongues ceased.

IV. WHY WOULD GOD USE TONGUES AS EVIDENCE?

(That is an amazing question!)

A. James 3 talks about the power of the tongue. It says it is the most unruly member, and the question came – can anyone tame it?

    1. When a person is speaking in other tongues, their tongue is yielded to the Holy Spirit. It does not have the ability to spew lies and deceit, wounds and hurts, but it is speaking Divine secrets, or praying for things in the Holy Spirit that will change lives. When one is speaking in tongues, that tongue becomes a life-giver and not something that produces death.

    2. Speaking in other tongues is one of the greatest ways to tame the tongue. And as the book of James declares, one who controls the tongue controls the whole body.

B. It is also a yielding to the supernatural. Many times, we want to be in complete control, do what we want to do, and say what we want to say. When we are speaking in other tongues, however, we are yielded to the supernatural and to God himself.

V. ARE TONGUES FOR TODAY?

A. One of the great confusions about speaking in other tongues is that many believe that it is a gift only given to a few. I have had people come to the church who have come from a Calvinistic background who actually now believe in tongues, but do not believe it is for everyone, but only those who have received that specific gift.

B. There is also the Calvinistic teaching that tongues ceased with the first century Church.

    1. This is the main verse they use to back up their understanding that tongues ceased with the Bible times.

        a. *1 Corinthians 13:8-10 Love never fails. But whether there are prophecies, they will fail; whether there are tongues, they will cease; whether there is knowledge, it will vanish away. ⁹For we know in part and we prophesy in part. ¹⁰But when that which is perfect has come, then that which is in part will be done away. NKJV*

        b. To truly understand the Scripture, you have to take it completely in context and not take out the portions you like and/or dislike. Let's take a look at the Scripture in its entirety, and see if you can take one portion out and leave the rest.

    2. Has KNOWLEDGE CEASED?

        a. "Since the early years of this century, the number of engineers has grown more than fivefold relative to population. Another measure of our increasing scientific knowledge is the growth of scientific journals. In the late 19th century there were about 5000 scientific journals, compared with the more than 60,000 that are today. In 1900 there were about 10,000 physics and electrical engineering abstracts. Now there are more than 250,000." ("It's getting better all the time: 100 and one great trends of the last 100 years", by Stephen).

3. Have PROPHECIES CEASED?

a. There are still prophecies that have to be fulfilled, even for the end times. The rapture has not yet occurred. The great tribulation period has not yet occurred. The millennial reign of Christ has not occurred. The Great White Throne Judgment has not yet occurred.

b. So my question to you would be – has prophecy ceased?

c. Have personal prophecies ceased?

d. According to 1 Corinthians Chapter 12, and the gifts of the Holy Spirit, prophecy is one of the gifts that is given to the Church.

e. Many people reading this have experienced the prophetic word from the Lord Jesus Christ through the gifts of the Holy Spirit. It has comforted, uplifted, encouraged, and enabled you to fight a greater warfare.

4. Has TONGUES CEASED?

a. If knowledge has not...

b. If prophecies have not...

c. Then why do people believe that tongues have?

d. Fear, misunderstanding, and abuse are all reasons, but you cannot throw the baby out with the bathwater.

e. Tongues have not ceased!

5. **Southern Baptist Convention stance:** Will Hall, spokesman for the SBC, says the denomination has no official policy on speaking in tongues for its churches or individual members. But there are signs the practice is gaining acceptance. Dallas Theological Seminary and Campus Crusade for Christ, two strongholds of independent Christianity, have done away with rich traditions on tongue-speaking for students and staff.
http://www.usatoday.com/news/health2007-05-23-tongues-brain_N.htm

VI. THE DIFFERENCE BETWEEN PUBLIC AND PRIVATE TONGUES

A. An area of confusion with the gift of tongues is that many do not believe they qualify, or that the Spirit wills them to be filled and speak in tongues.

B. There is a major difference between public tongues and private tongues, and when you do not understand the difference, it brings a lot of confusion. So let's fix the confusion by bringing understanding.

1. Public tongues:

a. *1 Corinthians 12:4-11 There are diversities of gifts, but the same Spirit. ⁵There are differences of ministries, but the same Lord. ⁶And there are diversities of activities, but it is the same God who works all in all. ⁷But the manifestation of the Spirit is given to each one for the profit of all: ⁸for to one is given the word of wisdom through the Spirit, to another the word of knowledge through the same Spirit, ⁹to another faith by the same Spirit, to another gifts of healings by the same Spirit, ¹⁰to another the working of miracles, to another prophecy, to another discerning of spirits, to **another different kinds of tongues, to another the interpretation of tongues.** ¹¹But one and the same Spirit works all these things, distributing to each one individually as He wills. NKJV*

b. The purpose for public tongues is to edify the whole body. The gifts of the Holy Spirit are for the purpose of building up and strengthening us. They are an avenue for God's voice to be heard by His body. It is a body experience, not an individual experience. It is for the whole, not just for the individual.

c. In the book of 1 Corinthians Chapter 14, we see Paul speaking to the Corinthian church about the abuse of the gifts of the Spirit in the church. The 14th chapter was written because the church was not working in the gifts properly, and Paul wasn't throwing out the gifts, or nullifying the gifts, but teaching them how to use the gifts of God properly.

d. 1 Corinthians 14:27-28 *If anyone speaks in a tongue, let there be two or at the most three, each in turn, and let one interpret. ²⁸But if there is no interpreter, let him keep silent in church, and let him speak to himself and to God. NKJV*

1) The reason Paul said this was not to stop tongues from being issued in the church. Confusion was being generated by many jumping up and speaking in tongues with no

interpretation. God is not the author of confusion, and wants order in His church. He was not stopping the gifts, just teaching about them.

2) Again, just because someone abuses something, doesn't mean you throw it away.

e. Public tongues are distributed by the Holy Spirit as He wills. This is when God wants to speak to his body publicly and vocally. The gifts of the Holy Spirit are available to every believer, but still, each believer is subject to the Holy Spirit as He desires to give edification to the body.

2. PRIVATE TONGUES / THE BAPTISM OF THE SPIRIT

a. Jesus told his disciples to go to Jerusalem and to wait till they receive the promise of a Father.

1) The purpose of the baptism of the Holy Spirit is not to speak in tongues. The purpose, however, is to impart more power to us.

2) We are not to be seeking the tongue, but the Baptizer! His name is Jesus.

b. The purpose of the baptism of the Holy Spirit is for more power.

1) *Acts 1:8 But you shall **receive power** when the Holy Spirit has come upon you; and you shall be witnesses to Me in Jerusalem, and in all Judea and Samaria, and to the end of the earth." NKJV*

2) The power is necessary to be a greater witness, to move in a stronger anointing, to move in the gifts of the Spirit, and to give greater evidence of the reality of God. We all need more power! Jesus has offered it; let's receive it.

c. When receiving the free gift of the baptism of the Holy Spirit, we have to remember that we are not after the tongue, but after the gift. The tongue is the initial evidence, but not the baptism.

1) I was recently in a service with Eddie James at His Tabernacle Family Church and he used a tremendous example that I would like to share with you. He said, "When you go to buy a shoe you do not go to buy the tongue, but the shoe. The tongue comes with the shoe, so don't seek the tongue, seek the shoe."

d. The purpose for private tongues:

1) First of all, it was the fulfillment of the prophecy found in Acts 2:15-21.

2) Private tongues **edifies oneself.**

a) *1 Corinthians 14:4 He who speaks in a tongue edifies himself, but he who prophesies edifies the church. NKJV*

b*) Jude 20 But you, beloved, building yourselves up on your most holy faith, praying in the Holy Spirit, NKJV*

3) Private tongues is a form of **intercession.**

a) *Romans 8:26 Likewise the Spirit also helps in our weaknesses. For we do not know what we should pray for as we ought, but the Spirit Himself makes intercession for us with groanings which cannot be uttered. NKJV*

4) Private tongues speak **Divine secrets and worship.**

a) *1 Corinthians 14:2 For he who speaks in a tongue does not speak to men but to God, for no one understands him; however, in the spirit he speaks mysteries. NKJV*

b) *Acts 2:11 Cretans and Arabs—we hear them speaking in our own tongues the wonderful works of God." NKJV*

c) *Acts 10:46 For they heard them speak with tongues and magnify God. NKJV*

VII. HOW DO I RECEIVE THE BAPTISM OF THE HOLY SPIRIT?

A. First of all, we have to understand that God wants us to receive the baptism. That it is Jesus' plan in today's world to be baptized in the Holy Spirit and to speak with other tongues.

1. *Acts 2:39 For the promise is to you and to your children, and to all who are afar off, as many as the Lord our God will call." NKJV*

2. The baptism of the Holy Spirit is a gift and it is free.

3. If you are saved, this gift is for you - "and to all who are afar off..."

B. Because it is a gift, that means you don't need to beg for it. You don't need to be perfect or jump through certain hoops; you just need to receive. In the same way you received salvation, that is how you receive the baptism of the Holy Spirit. When it becomes anything else, it is no longer a gift. Many churches make you feel like you have to beg for it or be perfect, but I'm willing to say it one more time - *a gift is a gift is a gift.*

1. I remember when I was in Bible school, and I was walking upstairs on the second floor of the dormitories. I passed a room with a young man who was praying out loud for the baptism of the Holy Spirit. He was begging and crying and asking Jesus to fill him. To some religious people, it sounded just right, but I knew that it was no longer a gift if you have to beg for it. I was eating a Tootsie Roll pop – raspberry flavor, which is my favorite – and had another one in my pocket. I walked into the room and asked him what he was doing. He said "Praying for the baptism of the Holy Spirit." I said, "You're working way too hard. It's this easy. Are you ready?" I handed him the other Tootsie Roll pop from my pocket and as he reached out for it, I said, "Receiving the baptism is that easy!" He unrolled the lollipop and put it in his mouth, and I said, "Take it out. We are going to receive the baptism the same way. Okay, ask now. No more English; pray in tongues!" He immediately began to speak with other tongues. It is that easy!

2. Can you imagine if on Christmas morning you ran downstairs to open your presents, but your parents made you beg for them before you could open them? You would think, *that's kind of sick!* Then why would God the Father do that to us when He has given us a free gift?

3. When you start to beg, when you start to plead, it no longer becomes a gift, so stop and just receive.

4. "What if I don't speak in tongues right away?" Don't worry about it; by faith receive, and you will begin to speak with other tongues.

C. PRAY WITH ME!

1. Jesus, I believe that you gave me a free gift called the baptism of the Holy Spirit. I am not seeking tongues, but I'm asking you to fill me with your Holy Spirit and with more power in Jesus' name. Right now, I receive my free gift in the name of Jesus. Amen.

a. Now just begin to speak with other tongues!

b. Jesus is not going to take it out and wag it; you must speak in faith what you are hearing in your head and your heart.

Chapter 3

Laying on of Hands

Hebrews 6:1-2
Therefore, leaving the discussion of the elementary principles of Christ, let us go on to perfection, not laying again the foundation of repentance from dead works and of faith toward God, ²of the doctrine of baptisms, of laying on of hands, of resurrection of the dead, and of eternal judgment. NKJV

I. LAYING ON OF HANDS

    A. The laying on of hands is a foundational principle.

        1. This principle has been lost in the local churches.

            a. Most people believe this is for the pastor, evangelist, or some special guests that visit the church.

            b. The truth is that this is for every single believer!

        2. The wisdom of the devil and the foolishness of the preachers have enabled the local churches to be powerless. Believers are seen more as pew sitters than men and women of war in the army of the Lord. Most believers do not even understand the basic principle of how to release the anointing. So first we need to understand the anointing, and then we will go back to the laying on of hands and learn how to release that anointing.

II. SO WHAT IS THE ANOINTING?

    A. First and foremost – the anointing is not the Holy Spirit.

        1. We sing about the anointing, we pray for the anointing, and we desire the anointing, but most Christians have no clue what the anointing is. This is so important for you to understand. If you do not understand the anointing, how do you know if you actually have it, or when you get it, or what are you going to do with it?

            a. *Isaiah 10:27 It shall come to pass in that day That his burden will be taken away from your shoulder, And his yoke from your neck, And the yoke will be destroyed because of the anointing oil. NKJV*

        2. The anointing is the energy or power that comes from the Holy Spirit to do supernatural works.

3. This enables a normal man to do work on behalf of the supernatural God!

4. When you and I go and get jobs, we expect that the company that we're going to be working for to have the equipment to do the job. If the company does not have the equipment to accomplish the job, then it would be absolute foolishness to work for them.

5. The anointing is the ability that God gives you and me to work for Him.

6. He not only tells us what to do, but He also gives us the ability, the energy, the supernatural ability, to accomplish heavenly tasks.

   a. He not only calls us; He equips us!

   b. *Zechariah 4:6 So he answered and said to me: "This is the word of the Lord to Zerubbabel:* **'Not by might nor by power, but by My Spirit,' Says the Lord of hosts.** *NKJV*

   c. Nothing eternal can be accomplished outside of the anointing.

B. The Old Testament Saints

   1. Not everybody was anointed in the Old Testament.

   2. There were only certain groups that were allowed to understand, experience, and use the anointing that destroys the yoke of bondage.

   3. The only people in the Old Testament that were anointed, are as follows:

      a. The Kings

         1) *Samuel 15:1 Samuel also said to Saul, "The Lord sent me to anoint you king over His people, over Israel. Now therefore, heed the voice of the words of the Lord. NKJV*

      b. The Priests

         1) *Exodus 40:13-15 You shall put the holy garments on Aaron, and anoint him and consecrate him, that he may minister to Me as priest.* ¹⁴*And you shall bring his sons and clothe them with tunics.* ¹⁵*You shall anoint them, as you anointed their father, that they may minister to Me as priests; for their anointing shall surely be an everlasting priesthood throughout their generations." NKJV*

c. The Prophets

> 1) *2 Kings 2:9-14 And so it was, when they had crossed over, that Elijah said to Elisha, "Ask! What may I do for you, before I am taken away from you?" Elisha said, "Please let a double portion of your spirit be upon me." ¹⁰So he said, "You have asked a hard thing. Nevertheless, if you see me when I am taken from you, it shall be so for you; but if not, it shall not be so." ¹¹Then it happened, as they continued on and talked, that suddenly a chariot of fire appeared with horses of fire, and separated the two of them; and Elijah went up by a whirlwind into heaven. ¹²And Elisha saw it, and he cried out, "My father, my father, the chariot of Israel and its horsemen!" So he saw him no more. And he took hold of his own clothes and tore them into two pieces. ¹³He also took up the mantle of Elijah that had fallen from him, and went back and stood by the bank of the Jordan. ¹⁴Then he took the mantle of Elijah that had fallen from him, and struck the water, and said, "Where is the Lord God of Elijah?" And when he also had struck the water, it was divided this way and that; and Elisha crossed over. NKJV*

> a) The mantle was another type of anointing.

d. The Builders of the Tabernacle

> 1) *Exodus 31:1-5 Then the Lord spoke to Moses, saying: ²"See, I have called by name Bezalel the son of Uri, the son of Hur, of the tribe of Judah. ³And I have filled him with the Spirit of God, in wisdom, in understanding, in knowledge, and in all manner of workmanship, ⁴to design artistic works, to work in gold, in silver, in bronze, ⁵in cutting jewels for setting, in carving wood, and to work in all manner of workmanship. NKJV*

4. The anointing only abided *in* the builders of the tabernacle. The Kings, the Priests, and the Prophets, all had the anointing *come upon* them, but the anointing did not abide *in* them.

a. The anointing came upon Samson.

> 1) *Judges 15:14 When he came to Lehi, the Philistines came shouting against him. Then **the Spirit of the Lord came mightily upon him**; and the ropes that were on his arms became like flax that is burned with fire, and his bonds broke loose from his hands. NKJV*

5. The anointing is tangible!

a. The word *tangible* means touchable, transferable.

b. The anointing was so strong in the prophet Elisha's bones that it raised a dead man.

> 1) *2 Kings 13:20-21 Then Elisha died, and they buried him. And the raiding bands from Moab invaded the land in the spring of the year. ²¹So it was, as they were burying a man, that suddenly they spied a band of raiders; and they put the man in the tomb of Elisha; and when the man was let down and touched the bones of Elisha, he revived and stood on his feet. NKJV*

C. What is amazing for us right now as New Testament believers is that Jesus is a mediator of a new and better covenant with better promises!

> 1. *Hebrews 8:6 But now He has obtained a more excellent ministry, inasmuch as He is also Mediator of a better covenant, which was established on better promises. NKJV*

> 2. The Old Testament saints had the anointing come upon them, but because of Jesus, we have the anointing abiding within us!

>> a. When we accept Jesus as our personal Savior, He comes in and lives in us by His Holy Spirit. We become temples of the Holy Ghost! That means you're possessed! Literally.

>> b. So that anointing abides within you because the Holy Spirit lives inside of you.

>> c. So in the Old Testament, the anointing come upon them, but as a New Testament saint, with a new and better promise, the anointing abides within and comes out of you, and can also come upon you.

D. Every believer is anointed.

> 1. *1 John 2:20 But you have an anointing from the Holy One, and you know all things. NKJV*

> 2. *1 John 2:27 But the anointing which you have received from Him abides in you, and you do not need that anyone teach you; but as the same anointing teaches you concerning all things, and is true, and is not a lie, and just as it has taught you, you will abide in Him. NKJV*

> 3. Jesus Himself did not do anything supernatural without the anointing.

a. God anointed Jesus to do the supernatural and produce good works.

> 1) *Acts 10:38 How God anointed Jesus of Nazareth with the Holy Spirit and with power, who went about doing good and healing all who were oppressed by the devil, for God was with Him. NKJV*

b. The Holy Spirit did not come upon Jesus until he was anointed. Then He was able to do supernatural exploits.

> 1) *Luke 3:21-23a When all the people were baptized, it came to pass that Jesus also was baptized; and while He prayed, the heaven was opened. ²²And the Holy Spirit descended in bodily form like a dove upon Him, and a voice came from heaven which said, "You are My beloved Son; in You I am well pleased." ²³Now Jesus Himself began His ministry at about thirty years of age. NKJV*

c. Jesus declared that the anointing was upon Him to do the work of God.

> 1) *Luke 4:18 "The Spirit of the Lord is upon Me, Because He has anointed Me To preach the gospel to the poor; He has sent Me to heal the brokenhearted, To proclaim liberty to the captives And recovery of sight to the blind, To set at liberty those who are oppressed; NKJV*

d. Jesus did not do miracles because He was the Son of God. He did miracles because He was the son of man, anointed by the Holy Spirit. He left all His heavenly glory and came down here to live as a normal man, with normal power, to show us that through the anointing, we can do everything He did.

> 1) *Philippians 2:5-7 Let this mind be in you which was also in Christ Jesus, ⁶who, being in the form of God, did not consider it robbery to be equal with God, ⁷but made Himself of no reputation, taking the form of a bondservant, and coming in the likeness of men. NKJV*

> 2) He was all God and all man in the same body. Yet He gave up all of His heavenly power so that He could show us how to work the works of God. Not from our own ability, but through the energy, anointing, and supernatural ability of God who lives inside of us; the Holy Ghost.

> 3) This is why Jesus said it would be better for Him to go away. When Jesus was on the planet, there was only one Jesus. Now

that Jesus rose from the dead, and is sitting at the right hand of the Father, He sent the Holy Spirit. This is the same Holy Spirit who dwelled inside of Jesus and now dwells inside of you.

> a) *Romans 8:11 But if the Spirit of Him who raised Jesus from the dead dwells in you, He who raised Christ from the dead will also give life to your mortal bodies through His Spirit who dwells in you. NKJV*

4) Now that the same Spirit dwells in you, you can do what Jesus did!

> a) *John 14:12 "Most assuredly, I say to you, he who believes in Me, the works that I do he will do also; and greater works than these he will do, because I go to My Father. NKJV*

E. HOW DO YOU INCREASE THE ANOINTING?

1. It is important to understand that you can measure the anointing.

   a. Jesus was anointed without measure.

   > 1) *John 3:34 For He whom God has sent speaks the words of God, for God does not give the Spirit by measure. NKJV*

   b. Elisha received a double portion.

   > 1) *2 Kings 2:9 And so it was, when they had crossed over, that Elijah said to Elisha, "Ask! What may I do for you, before I am taken away from you?" Elisha said, "Please let a double portion of your spirit be upon me." NKJV*

2. Every Christian is anointed, but what is even more powerful is when you get in the corporate anointing. This is called synergy. Psalms 133 declares that the commanded blessing is in the corporate anointing.

3. The disciples were anointed in the Gospels, but that anointing was the Old Testament principle where the Spirit came upon them. Before Jesus was taken away, He knew they would need more power, so He told them to go to Jerusalem and wait for the Promise of the Father.

4. If you desire to increase the anointing in your life, there are certain things that need to be accomplished.

   a. Be filled with the Holy Spirit.

1) *Acts 1:8 But you shall receive power when the Holy Spirit has come upon you; and you shall be witnesses to Me in Jerusalem, and in all Judea and Samaria, and to the end of the earth." NKJV*

2) *Acts 2:4 And they were all filled with the Holy Spirit and began to speak with other tongues, as the Spirit gave them utterance. NKJV*

    a) Please refer back to Chapter 2 for more information on the Baptism in the Holy Spirit with the evidence of speaking with other tongues.

3) Jesus never did anything just to do it. He always had a plan. When Jesus sent His disciples to tarry in Jerusalem until they received the Promise of the Father, He knew what they were going for. It wasn't just to have a meeting, or to have a little church, but to receive something they needed to fulfill the purpose of the kingdom. Jesus sent them to the upper room because they needed more power to accomplish the purpose of God.

4) So to increase the anointing in your life, you need to be filled with the Holy Spirit to have more power.

5) Then get refilled!

    a) *Acts 4:27-31 "For truly against Your holy Servant Jesus, whom You anointed, both Herod and Pontius Pilate, with the Gentiles and the people of Israel, were gathered together 28to do whatever Your hand and Your purpose determined before to be done. 29Now, Lord, look on their threats, and grant to Your servants that with all boldness they may speak Your word, 30by stretching out Your hand to heal, and that signs and wonders may be done through the name of Your holy Servant Jesus." 31And when they had prayed, the place where they were assembled together was shaken; and they were all filled with the Holy Spirit, and they spoke the word of God with boldness. NKJV*

b. Speak in tongues all the time.

    1) 1 Corinthians 14:2 – Speaking divine secrets.

    2) 1 Corinthians 14:4 – Encouraging yourself.

3) Jude 20 – Building yourself up.

4) When you pray in tongues, you are speaking spirit to Spirit. Your focus is on the things above, not on the things below.

c. Just do it!

1) Do you remember when your child first started driving and you had to teach them? You make sure your seat belt was really tight. Your foot went to the floor like you had a brake on your own side. If you could grab the wheel, you would have, and in more than one instance, you were scared to death! When your child started driving, they weren't that good. They had to learn distance, depth perception, and simply just how to turn the wheel at the right time. It wasn't until they started to practice that they started to understand and become good at what they were doing. Why should we think learning how to flow in the anointing and to move in the power of God is any different? If you never practice, you will never learn!

a) *Hebrews 5:14 But solid food belongs to those who are of full age, that is, those who by reason of use have their senses exercised to discern both good and evil. NKJV*

b) *Matthew 10:7-8 And as you go, preach, saying, 'The kingdom of heaven is at hand.' ⁸Heal the sick, cleanse the lepers, raise the dead, cast out demons. Freely you have received, freely give. NKJV*

c) *Mark 16:15-20 And He said to them, "Go into all the world and preach the gospel to every creature. ¹⁶He who believes and is baptized will be saved; but he who does not believe will be condemned. ¹⁷And these signs will follow those who believe: In My name they will cast out demons; they will speak with new tongues; ¹⁸they will take up serpents; and if they drink anything deadly, it will by no means hurt them; they will lay hands on the sick, and they will recover." ¹⁹So then, after the Lord had spoken to them, He was received up into heaven, and sat down at the right hand of God. ²⁰And they went out and preached everywhere, the Lord working with them and confirming the word through the accompanying signs. Amen. NKJV*

2) Let's say you buy a brand-new Lamborghini. It's red, it's fast, and you can't wait to get behind the wheel. You drive it out of the dealership, take it to the gas station, put high-octane gasoline in it, drive it to your garage, and park it. How crazy would it be if you never drove that car again? It's got all the power it needs and all the fuel it needs, but if you don't use it, it's worthless.

3) The more you give, the more you increase!

F. RELEASING THE ANOINTING

1. We are finally here - the laying on of hands.

2. Releasing the anointing can be done in various ways. According to the book of Hebrews chapter 6, there is a fundamental and foundational principle in the releasing of the anointing. This is called the laying on of hands. Remember, this is elementary. This is just the beginning, so learning how to lay hands on people and releasing the presence and power of God through the laying on of hands is just the beginning.

   a. The basic understanding of the laying on of hands to release the anointing is that you and I are conduits of the power of God. Think of it in this manner – if you wanted to turn the lights on in the house, there would have to be wires coming from the transformer on the pole to the house. When the wires come into the house, they would have to go to a panel box. From the panel box, wires are distributed throughout the house and end at a light switch or plug. When you flick the light switch, the energy – the power – is released to that room.

   b. God's heavenly, supernatural energy is waiting to be released through us as his conduits to this world. When we lay hands on somebody and release the power of God, it is like turning on that light switch.

   c. **Jesus used the principles of laying hands on people to release the power of God.**

      1) *Matthew 8:14-15 Now when Jesus had come into Peter's house, He saw his wife's mother lying sick with a fever. 15So He touched her hand, and the fever left her. And she arose and served them. NKJV*

      2) *Matthew 8:3 Then Jesus put out His hand and touched him, saying, "I am willing; be cleansed." Immediately his leprosy was cleansed. NKJV*

d. **Speaking the Word is another way to release the anointing.**

> 1) *Matthew 8:5-10 Now when Jesus had entered Capernaum, a centurion came to Him, pleading with Him, ⁶saying, "Lord, my servant is lying at home paralyzed, dreadfully tormented." ⁷And Jesus said to him, "I will come and heal him." ⁸The centurion answered and said, "Lord, I am not worthy that You should come under my roof. But only speak a word, and my servant will be healed. ⁹For I also am a man under authority, having soldiers under me. And I say to this one, 'Go,' and he goes; and to another, 'Come,' and he comes; and to my servant, 'Do this,' and he does it."¹⁰When Jesus heard it, He marveled, and said to those who followed, "Assuredly, I say to you, I have not found such great faith, not even in Israel! NKJV*

e. **The anointing can be transferred tangibly, through objects.**

> 1) *Acts 19:11-12 Now God worked unusual miracles by the hands of Paul, ¹²so that even handkerchiefs or aprons were brought from his body to the sick, and the diseases left them and the evil spirits went out of them. NKJV*

> 2) There was an evangelist who was getting ready to preach the Word of God and a woman ran up to him and gave him a piece of candy. He looked at her and said, "Thank you very much." She said, "No, no, you don't understand. That's not for you. My sister is in an insane asylum, and they steal everything from her except her candy. I want you to suck on the candy now and then again after you preach, and then I'll send it to my sister so she can be free from those demons." After service, she ran up and got the candy and sent it to her sister. Within 10 days, she was completely free and in her right mind and she was released from the asylum.

> 3) When I was in Bible school, Ted Shuttlesworth came and had some services. The pastor of the church at the Bible school was a very boring preacher, and the students used to make fun of him. Ted Shuttlesworth stood up and declared, "Some of you students are making fun of this old man, but he has more anointing in his coat than you have in your whole life. If you want a portion of the anointing, get up here." Brother Shuttlesworth held one arm of the coat, and the pastor held its other arm. Anyone who wanted the anointing needed to go underneath that coat. I was the first in line, and when we hit that coat, the power of God was released, the energy of heaven

let loose, and people's lives were changed. There were 500 people either dancing or out in the Holy Ghost when they hit that coat. I witnessed that myself.

4) One evangelist used to send out newsletters to his supporters. He prayed over those newsletters and then sent them out anointed of the Holy Spirit. A lady in Africa received her newsletter and when she did, the anointing healed her body through that tangible anointing.

f. Spitting

1) I know this one is not popular, but Jesus did it more than once. If you do this these days, you'd better know God!

a) *Mark 7:33-35 And He took him aside from the multitude, and put His fingers in his ears, and He spat and touched his tongue. [34]Then, looking up to heaven, He sighed, and said to him, "Ephphatha ," that is, "Be opened." [35]Immediately his ears were opened, and the impediment of his tongue was loosed, and he spoke plainly. NKJV*

2) One day when I was listening to some great stories of evangelists that traveled America, I heard this story about the spitting evangelist. When he would pray for people, he would spit on them, and miraculously, they would be healed. One day, he was preaching in the back hills of America and he came upon a man who was born with one arm shorter than the other. The short arm only came down to where the elbow would be. He spit on that arm, laid hands on the man, and commanded the arm to grow. In front of everyone, the arm supernaturally grew to the normal length with a hand on the end!

3) I guess if you really need a miracle, it doesn't really matter how you get it, as long as you get it.

g. Shadow

1) *Acts 5:14-15 And believers were increasingly added to the Lord, multitudes of both men and women, [15]so that they brought the sick out into the streets and laid them on beds and couches, that at least the shadow of Peter passing by might fall on some of them. NKJV*

h. **Point of contact**

1) There are so many ways to release the anointing. It is that point of contact, the point of faith in the release of the energy of heaven that abides within you.

2) Smith Wigglesworth punched people, at times. Harfouche mentioned A.A. Allen and Smith Wigglesworth as great men. He then tells a story of how he was shocked at what they would do under the anointing. But the "Holy" Spirit was telling him to do the same! He related a story about how God spoke to him to punch a woman in her deteriorating jaw. So he punched her in the face. She hit the floor out cold, and when she came to, she was healed by the power of God. He punched another in the stomach and healed a tumor. I'd hate to think what he'd do to an impotent person. This is suspiciously similar to Kenneth Hagin's *tales of the spirit*. And why not, the Rodney Browne connection to Hagin is there. If you can find in the Bible any apostle physically doing such a thing to anyone, please inform me on this. Harfouche does seem to take the Wigglesworth approach – a "woman in tormenting pain came up for prayer. Her back was deteriorating. I said, "Turn around and show me where it is." When I said that, the pastor knew I was going to hit her in the back. His wife knew I was going to hit her in the back. And my wife knew I was going to hit her in the back. Later, the pastor told me, "I almost stopped you and said, 'Don't hit her in the back! She's in a lot of pain.'" But before he could talk me out of it, I had hit her in the back, and she was completely healed by the power of God! Why? Because there is a "knowing" that can operate in you." (The Miracle Ministry of the Prophet p. 93)

These are very powerful stories and examples of the releasing of the anointing of the Holy Spirit, but remember, you must start in elementary school, and that is the laying on of hands. Start laying hands on everybody and anything and releasing that anointing. I've seen animals healed, cars healed, and people even laying hands on themselves and being healed.

If you never start, you will never get out of elementary school!

Chapter 4

The Rapture of the Church and the Resurrections

Hebrews 6:1-2
Therefore, leaving the discussion of the elementary principles of Christ, let us go on to perfection, not laying again the foundation of repentance from dead works and of faith toward God, ²of the doctrine of baptisms, of laying on of hands, of resurrection of the dead, and of eternal judgment. NKJV

I. RESURRECTION OF THE DEAD

A. This next stone of our foundation has multiple parts that we are going to want to investigate.

    1. There is more than one resurrection!

    2. We will not count Jesus rising from the dead on the third day.

        a. *Matthew 28:5-8 But the angel answered and said to the women, "Do not be afraid, for I know that you seek Jesus who was crucified. ⁶He is not here; for He is risen, as He said. Come, see the place where the Lord lay. ⁷And go quickly and tell His disciples that He is risen from the dead, and indeed He is going before you into Galilee; there you will see Him. Behold, I have told you." NKJV*

        b. Jesus is the first fruits of the resurrection.

            1) *1 Corinthians 15:20 But now Christ is risen from the dead, and has become the first fruits of those who have fallen asleep. NKJV*

    3. So Jesus is the first resurrection from the dead!

B. There is a need to understand the history of mankind from the beginning to the end.

    1. At the end of this chapter there is a chart of the history of the Bible.

    2. Let's look at it and learn about the history, which will bring an understanding of the resurrections and judgments.

C. The basic history of man and life after death.

1. When Adam and Eve sinned in the garden, the whole separation process began. Up to this point, Adam and Eve walked with God daily and spent time in His presence.

2. When sin came on the scene, there was a separation from the presence of God since no sin can be in His presence.

> a. *Genesis 3:8-9 And they heard the sound of the Lord God walking in the garden in the cool of the day, and Adam and his wife hid themselves from the presence of the Lord God among the trees of the garden. ⁹Then the Lord God called to Adam and said to him, "Where are you?" NKJV*

>> 1) My personal opinion is that these are the saddest verses in the Bible. God is all-knowing, so why did He ask where Adam was? It was not the physical location that was missing, but that intimate relationship that was now breached.

>> 2) So up to this point, man was not supposed to die physically, but because of sin, man would now die physically until the judgments.

3. At this point, when man died, he went to either one of two places.

> a. Both of these places are what we will call, "HOLDING TANKS."

> b. Abraham's Bosom

>> 1) This is where the righteous Old Testament saints went when they died. It was not heaven because the blood that was shed in the Old Covenant only covered the sins of the people. It was not until Jesus that the sins were washed completely away.

>> 2) This was a place where the children of God could communicate with each other. It was a place of peace.

>>> a) *Luke 16:19-31 "There was a certain rich man who was clothed in purple and fine linen and fared sumptuously every day. ²⁰But there was a certain beggar named Lazarus, full of sores, who was laid at his gate, ²¹desiring to be fed with the crumbs which fell from the rich man's table. Moreover the dogs came and licked his sores. ²²So it was that the beggar died, and was carried by the angels to Abraham's bosom. The rich man also died and was buried. ²³And being in torments in Hades, he lifted up his eyes and saw Abraham afar off, and Lazarus in his bosom.²⁴"Then he cried and said, 'Father Abraham, have*

mercy on me, and send Lazarus that he may dip the tip of his finger in water and cool my tongue; for I am tormented in this flame.' ²⁵But Abraham said, 'Son, remember that in your lifetime you received your good things, and likewise Lazarus evil things; but now he is comforted and you are tormented. ²⁶And besides all this, between us and you there is a great gulf fixed, so that those who want to pass from here to you cannot, nor can those from there pass to us.'²⁷"Then he said, 'I beg you therefore, father, that you would send him to my father's house, ²⁸for I have five brothers, that he may testify to them, lest they also come to this place of torment.' ²⁹Abraham said to him, 'They have Moses and the prophets; let them hear them.' ³⁰And he said, 'No, father Abraham; but if one goes to them from the dead, they will repent.' ³¹But he said to him, 'If they do not hear Moses and the prophets, neither will they be persuaded though one rise from the dead.'" NKJV

3) Abraham's Bosom ceased being a holding tank when Jesus died and rose from the dead.

    a) *Ephesians 4:8 Therefore He says: "When He ascended on high, He led captivity captive, And gave gifts to men." NKJV*

    b) At this point, those in the bosom were WASHED in the blood and completely purified so they could be in the literal presence of the Father.

    c) Now when a Christian dies, they go right into the presence of the Lord and there is no holding tank because of Jesus.

        i. *2 Corinthians 5:8 We are confident, yes, well pleased rather to be absent from the body and to be present with the Lord. NKJV*

c. Hell

1) This is the HOLDING TANK for the unrighteous.

2) This is a place of torment for those who rejected God and His principles.

3) See above for description (Luke 16:19-31).

4) To this day and until the FINAL JUDGMENT hell is still the holding tank for sinners who are not washed in the blood of Jesus.

5) So when a person dies today, and they do not know Jesus, they do not soul sleep or party, but are separated and tormented by the god they chose to serve; Satan.

6) This will not cease to be the holding tank until Revelation 20:11-15, the White Throne Judgment of the sinner.

4. This is a great place to say – There is No Purgatory.

a. 1140 AD - The **doctrine** of **purgatory** was partly introduced towards the end of the fifth century, and revived by Gregory the Great in the sixth century; but it was never positively affirmed till the year **1140**, nor made an article of faith till the council of Trent. http://www.google.com/search?q=doctrine+of+purgatory&hl=en&client=safari&rls=en-us&sa=X&tbs=tl:1&tbo=u&ei=x455SsSuGI61tgeI2pnMAQ&oi=timeline_result&ct=title&resnum=11

b. 1031 The Church gives the name Purgatory to this final purification of the elect, which is entirely different from the punishment of the damned.[604] The Church formulated her doctrine of faith on Purgatory, especially at the Councils of Florence and Trent. The tradition of the Church, by reference to certain texts of Scripture, speaks of a cleansing fire: http://christianity.about.com/gi/dynamic/offsite.htm?zi=1/XJ&sdn=christianity&cdn=religion&tm=60&f=10&tt=29&bt=0&bts=0&zu=http%3A//www.christusrex.org/www1/CDHN/art12.html%23FINAL

c. 1032 This teaching is also based on the practice of prayer for the dead, already mentioned in Sacred Scripture: "Therefore Judas Maccabeus] made atonement for the dead, that they might be delivered from their sin."[607] From the beginning the Church has honored the memory of the dead and offered prayers in suffrage for them, above all the Eucharistic sacrifice, so that, thus purified, they may attain the beatific vision of God.[608] The Church also commends almsgiving, indulgences, and works of penance undertaken on behalf of the dead: http://christianity.about.com/gi/dynamic/offsite.htm?zi=1/XJ&sdn=christianity&cdn=religion&tm=60&f=10&tt=29&bt=0&bts=0&zu=http%3A//www.christusrex.org/www1/CDHN/art12.html%23FINAL

d. This doctrine has no Biblical proof and was created by the Catholic Church. They do use one verse out of the Apocrypha, and one out of 1 Corinthians 3:11-5, but the Apocrypha is not recognized as a part of the Canon, and the portion in 1 Corinthians is talking about the Bema Seat of Christ (Judgment of the Christians).

D. The Second Resurrection

1. This is what is termed, the RAPTURE OF THE CHURCH.

2. Methods of Interpretation:

a. Spiritualization – This is the type of interpretation that says that all Scripture has or can be made into a spiritual application. That it does not matter what the original writer meant, but it could mean something different today because of the spiritual times.

b. Historical, grammar interpretation – This type says that we must understand history, grammar, and the customs of the times to know what the literal interpretation was meant to be. That you cannot just make a text say what you want, but the context determines the interpretation; the literal interpretation of the Scripture.

II. **Pre-Tribulationalism**

A. Jesus will be coming BEFORE the Great Tribulation.

1. 1 Thessalonians 4:16-18

2. The word *rapture* is not in the Bible. The principle is "the taking away."

3. The principle of *imminence* means that Jesus can come at any moment.

4. There is not one prophecy left to be fulfilled before Jesus comes back.

B. The Holy Spirit is the restrainer on the earth.

1. 2 Thessalonians 2:3 – The Holy Spirit is the one who is holding back the satanic powers. When the Spirit and the salt are removed from the earth then Satan can do what he desires.

a. "The lawless one cannot be revealed until the Restrainer is removed."

C. There is a difference between the rapture and the Second Coming.

1. The rapture is when Jesus comes in the clouds and takes His people home (Acts 1:9-11).

2. The Second Coming is when Jesus will actually come and touch the Mount of Olives (Rev. 19:11-16).

D. The Church is different from Israel.

1. Israel has a different place in end time prophecy. One of the purposes of the great tribulation is to draw the Israelites back to Christ. All the events of the end times are centralized in Israel.

a. The Temple is being rebuilt.

b. The 144,000 witnesses are 12,000 people from each tribe who go around and share Jesus (Revelation 7:4-9).

c. The two witnesses (Revelation 11) are killed in Israel and resurrected after 3 ½ days.

2. The Church is the body of Christ. This body was not created until the death and resurrection of the Messiah.

a. The Church is addressed in Revelation 2-3 through the 7 churches that are being spoken to prophetically through John the Revelator.

1) Five of the churches were condemned.

2) Two were commended.

3) Most scholars believe that Laodicean Church represents the apostate church of the last days (Revelation 3:14-22).

b. After chapter 3, we do not see the church again until Revelation 19 when Jesus comes for the Second Coming and the battle of Armageddon.

c. The Twenty-Four Elders – Revelation 4:4

1) They are clothed in white raiment.

2) They are crowned with golden crowns.

3) They are in heaven in the presence of God.

4) They cannot be angels:

a) Crowned (Stephanos) – received as rewards.

b) They are seated on thrones – This was promised (Revelation 3:21).

c) The Testimony – Sing a new song about the blood (Revelation 5:9-10).

d) Twenty-four is the number of choruses into which the Levitical priesthood was divided (1 Chronicles 24:1-19).

III. **Mid-Tribulationalism**

A. This belief says that the Church will be raptured halfway through the great tribulation.

B. They believe that the first 3 ½ years of the Tribulation are not great wrath (seals and the trumpets), but that the last 3 ½ years will manifest wrath.

1. They deny the separation between Israel and the Church.

2. They believe that the Tribulation period is divided into two distinct sections. The two are unrelated and that is how the church can go through the first half, but cannot go through the second.

3. They deny that Jesus can come back at any second. He can be timed by what the details are of the first 3 ½ years.

4. They spiritualize the Scripture.

a. They say the rapture is depicted in Revelation 11, that the trumpet being blown is that of 1 Thessalonians 4:16-18.

b. 7 seals & 7 trumpets = first half of tribulation (Ch. 4-11).

c. 7 bowls = the last half of the tribulation.

5. The literal and chronological interpretation says:

a. 7 seals = first 3 ½ years (Ch. 4-7).

b. 7 trumpets = last 3 ½ years (Ch. 8-11)

c. Second Coming (Ch. 11:15-18).

d. 7 bowls = closing the age.

IV. Post-Tribulationalism

A. They have no distinction between Israel and the church.

B. They deny the purpose and nature of the tribulation.

C. They make the rapture and the Second Coming the same event.

D. They deny that Daniel is prophetic.

E. They apply Scriptures meant for Israel to the church.

F. The third Resurrection is that of the Old Testament Saints & Martyred Saints.

1. There is the resurrection of tribulation martyrs and Old Testament saints at the end of the tribulation period.

2. Martyrs of the tribulation – Revelation 20:4

a. *Revelation 20:4 And I saw thrones, and they sat on them, and judgment was committed to them. Then I saw the souls of those who had been beheaded for their witness to Jesus and for the word of God, who had not worshiped the beast or his image, and had not received his mark on their foreheads or on their hands. And they lived and reigned with Christ for a thousand years. NKJV*

3. Old Testament Saints – Daniel 12:1-2; Isaiah 26:19; Job 19:25-26

a. *Daniel 12:1-2 "At that time Michael shall stand up, The great prince who stands watch over the sons of your people; And there shall be a time of trouble, Such as never was since there was a nation, Even to that time. And at that time your people shall be delivered, Every one who is found written in the book. ²And many of those who sleep in the dust of the earth shall awake, Some to everlasting life, Some to shame and everlasting contempt. NKJV*

b. *Isaiah 26:19 Your dead shall live; Together with my dead body they shall arise. Awake and sing, you who dwell in dust; For your dew is like the dew of herbs, And the earth shall cast out the dead. NKJV*

c. *Job 19:25-26 For I know that my Redeemer lives, And He shall stand at last on the earth; ²⁶And after my skin is destroyed, this I know, That in my flesh I shall see God, NKJV*

d. When interpreting the Word of God according to the due process of hermeneutics, these verses cannot be taken figuratively, but must be understood literally.

e. The martyred tribulation saints and the Old Testament saints are the final resurrection of the people of God. The final resurrection will be that of the unsaved at the White Throne Judgment.

f. The martyred tribulation saints and the OT saints will finally have their physical bodies resurrected so they can be granted the eternal bodies that Jesus already gave those who were resurrected during the rapture.

V. The Fourth and Final Resurrection

A. The final resurrection is that of the unsaved.

B. Up to this point, all the unsaved dead have been stored in the holding tank called hell.

1. The final resurrection is for just one purpose. Those whose names are not written in the Lamb's Book of Life will be the resurrected.

2. *Revelation 20:11-15 Then I saw a great white throne and Him who sat on it, from whose face the earth and the heaven fled away. And there was found no place for them. 12And I saw the dead, small and great, standing before God, and books were opened. And another book was opened, which is the Book of Life. And the dead were judged according to their works, by the things which were written in the books. 13**The sea gave up the dead who were in it, and Death and Hades delivered up the dead who were in them**. And they were judged, each one according to his works. 14Then Death and Hades were cast into the lake of fire. This is the second death. 15And anyone not found written in the Book of Life was cast into the lake of fire. NKJV*

3. This resurrection is so those who are dead (the first death), and in Hades (the holding tank), will be resurrected with their bodies and will stand before God at the White Throne Judgment.

VI. What kind of body will we have when we are resurrected?

A. The Christians will receive a GLORIFIED body according to the Word of God.

1. *1 Corinthians 15:42-53 So also is the resurrection of the dead. The body is sown in corruption, it is raised in incorruption. 43It is sown in dishonor, it is raised in glory. It is sown in weakness, it is raised in power. 44It is sown a*

*natural body, it is raised a spiritual body. There is a natural body, and there is a spiritual body. ⁴⁵And so it is written, "The first man Adam became a living being." The last Adam became a life-giving spirit. ⁴⁶However, the spiritual is not first, but the natural, and afterward the spiritual. ⁴⁷The first man was of the earth, made of dust; the second Man is the Lord from heaven. ⁴⁸As was the man of dust, so also are those who are made of dust; and as is the heavenly Man, so also are those who are heavenly. ⁴⁹And as we have borne the image of the man of dust, we shall also bear the image of the heavenly Man.⁵⁰Now this I say, brethren, that flesh and blood cannot inherit the kingdom of God; nor does corruption inherit incorruption. ⁵¹Behold, I tell you a mystery: We shall not all sleep, but we shall all be changed— ⁵²in a moment, in the twinkling of an eye, at the last trumpet. For the trumpet will sound, and **the dead will be raised incorruptible, and we shall be changed. ⁵³For this corruptible must put on incorruption, and this mortal must put on immortality.** NKJV*

2. *Philippians 3:20-21 For our citizenship is in heaven, from which we also eagerly wait for the Savior, the Lord Jesus Christ, ²¹who will transform our lowly body that it may be conformed to His glorious body, according to the working by which He is able even to subdue all things to Himself. NKJV*

    a. We will have the body of Christ.

    b. On earth, life is in the blood, but in heaven, life is in the Father.

        1) *Leviticus 17:11 For the life of the flesh is in the blood. NKJV*

        2) Our physical bodies are not eternal now because of the sin of Adam and Eve.

        3) Our bodies were constructed to be eternal and were not made to break down and age like they do today, but sin brought death; both spiritual and physical.

            a) *Genesis 3:4-5 Then the serpent said to the woman, "You will not surely die. ⁵For God knows that in the day you eat of it your eyes will be opened, and you will be like God, knowing good and evil." NKJV*

            b) They did not physically die immediately, but the body was doomed from that point.

    c. The new body of incorruption means that it will not decay or die.

        1) Jesus received this body after He rose from the dead.

            a) This new body was touchable.

i. *John 20:29 The other disciples therefore said to him, "We have seen the Lord." So he said to them, "Unless I see in His hands the print of the nails, and put my finger into the print of the nails, and put my hand into His side, I will not believe." NKJV*

b) Jesus was able to go through walls.

i. *John 20:19-20 Then, the same day at evening, being the first day of the week, when the doors were shut where the disciples were assembled, for fear of the Jews, **Jesus came and stood in the midst**, and said to them, "Peace be with you." 20When He had said this, He showed them His hands and His side. Then the disciples were glad when they saw the Lord. NKJV*

ii. Beam me up, Scotty! That is so stinking cool!

c) Jesus was recognized, so our new bodies will be recognizable by others that we know.

d) Jesus was able to eat with His new body.

i. *John 21:12-13 Jesus said to them, "Come and eat breakfast." Yet none of the disciples dared ask Him, "Who are You?"—knowing that it was the Lord. 13Jesus then came and took the bread and gave it to them, and likewise the fish. NKJV*

B. The unbelievers will also receive an eternal body.

1. Every person on this planet is eternal and will live throughout all eternity.

2. The unbeliever will experience eternal suffering, yet their bodies will not be consumed.

3. This is called the second death.

a. *Revelation 20:14-15 Then Death and Hades were cast into the lake of fire. **This is the second death**. 15And anyone not found written in the Book of Life was cast into the lake of fire. NKJV*

4. We know according to Luke 16:24, *"Then he cried and said, 'Father Abraham, have mercy on me, and send Lazarus that he may dip the tip of his finger in water and cool my tongue; for I am tormented in this flame.' NKJV*

    a. *Matthew 13:41-42 The Son of Man will send out His angels, and they will gather out of His kingdom all things that offend, and those who practice lawlessness, 42 and will cast them into the furnace of fire. There will be wailing and gnashing of teeth. NKJV*

5. For all eternity, they will be alive, feel and sense pain, and have emotions.

This concludes the resurrections that are found in the Word of God that will establish a stone in your spiritual foundation.

Biblical Timeline

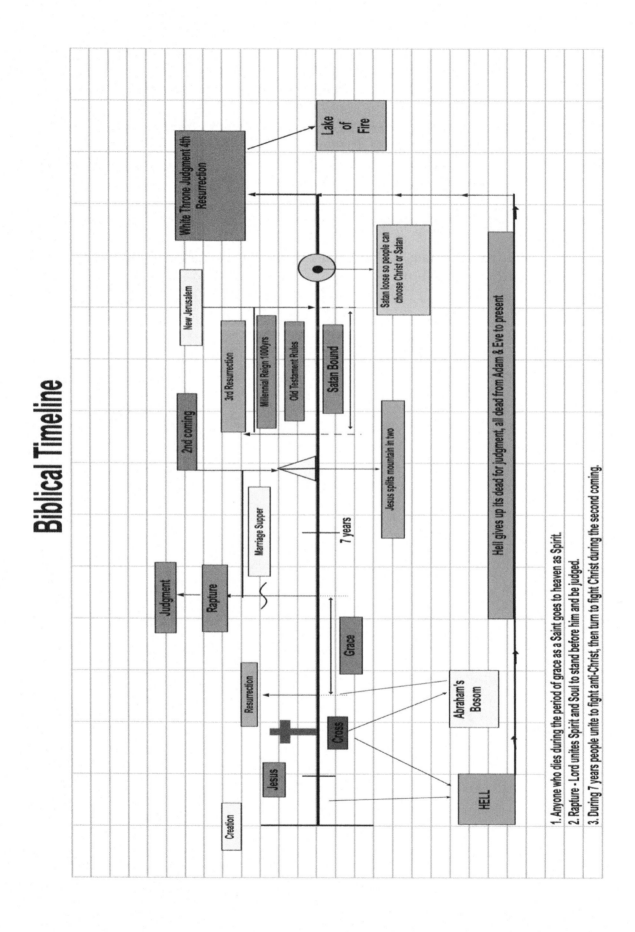

1. Anyone who dies during the period of grace as a Saint goes to heaven as Spirit.
2. Rapture - Lord unites Spirit and Soul to stand before him and be judged.
3. During 7 years people unite to fight anti-Christ, then turn to fight Christ during the second coming.

44

Chapter 5

Judgments

Hebrews 6:1-2
Therefore, leaving the discussion of the elementary principles of Christ, let us go on to perfection, not laying again the foundation of repentance from dead works and of faith toward God, ²of the doctrine of baptisms, of laying on of hands, of resurrection of the dead, and of eternal judgment. NKJV

I. Judgment of the Saint and the Sinner

A. *Hebrews 9:27 And as it is appointed for men to die once, but after this the judgment, NKJV*

1. Every single human being is going to be judged by a RIGHTEOUS, JUST, POWERFUL GOD.

B. It is important to understand judgment because a Christian will not be judged the same way a sinner is judged.

1. Most Christians do not understand this foundation and because of that, they have a strange fear of God (not healthy) because they believe they can still go to the Lake of Fire.

2. So let's get into the Word and break down the understanding of the two different judgments; one for the Saint, and one for the Sinner.

II. Judgment of the Saint

A. In the Bible, the judgment of the Saint occurs just after the rapture of the Church.

1. Speaking as a pre-tribulationalist it would happen on this time schedule:

a. The trumpet will sound (1 Thessalonians 4:16-18).

b. The rapture of the body of Christ commences.

1) The dead in Christ will rise first.

2) Then the living Saints will rise from the earth.

c. In the air (firmament – the space between heaven and earth), the Bema Seat of Christ will begin.

1) The Bema Seat or Judgment Seat of Christ.

    a) *Romans 14:10 But why do you judge your brother? Or why do you show contempt for your brother? For we shall all stand before the judgment seat of Christ. NKJV*

    b) *2 Corinthians 5:10 For we must all appear before the judgment seat of Christ, that each one may receive the things done in the body, according to what he has done, whether good or bad. NKJV*

B. As a Christian, you will not be judged for your sin!

    1. Jesus has washed your sins away and you are a son or daughter of the Most High.

        a. *1 John 1:9 If we confess our sins, He is faithful and just to forgive us our sins and to cleanse us from all unrighteousness. NKJV*

        b. *Psalms 103:12 As far as the east is from the west, So far has He removed our transgressions from us. NKJV*

        c. God does not hold your forgiven sin against you and you will not be judged for those sins. They are under the blood of Jesus and cannot and will not be held over your head.

    2. So if I am not being judged for my sin, then what will I be judged for?

        a. *1 Corinthians 3:11-15 For no other foundation can anyone lay than that which is laid, which is Jesus Christ. ¹²Now if anyone builds on this foundation with gold, silver, precious stones, wood, hay, straw, ¹³**each one's work will become clear**; for the Day will declare it, because it will be revealed by fire; and the fire will test each one's work, of what sort it is. ¹⁴**If anyone's work which he has built on it endures, he will receive a reward**. ¹⁵If anyone's work is burned, he will suffer loss; but he himself will be saved, yet so as through fire. NKJV*

            1) As Christians, we will be judged for the works that we have done for the Kingdom of God.

                a) *1 Corinthians 3:8 Now he who plants and he who waters are one, and each one will receive his own reward according to his own labor. NKJV*

            2) Only the things that are done for Christ will last.

3) Our purpose on this earth is not just to make money, have a career, and live in a nice house. Those are all temporary things that will not have validity as we are being judged.

> a) *2 Corinthians 4:18 while we do not look at the things which are seen, but at the things which are not seen. For the things which are seen are temporary, but the things which are not seen are eternal. NKJV*

4) We have been purposed by God; we have been commissioned, sent, appointed, and propelled as His children to do the will of the Father.

5) We were not saved just to go to heaven or we would already be there.

6) You have been saved to fulfill a purpose that you and only you have been given. There is nobody on this planet like you. You are special and planned by God Himself to accomplish a mission that you only can accomplish in Him.

> a) *Psalms 139:14 I will praise You, for I am fearfully and wonderfully made; Marvelous are Your works, And that my soul knows very well. NKJV*

> b) Jeremiah 1:4-5 *Then the word of the Lord came to me, saying: 5"Before I formed you in the womb I knew you; Before you were born I sanctified you; I ordained you a prophet to the nations." NKJV*

> c) *John 15:16 You did not choose Me, but I chose you and appointed you that you should go and bear fruit, and that your fruit should remain, that whatever you ask the Father in My name He may give you. NKJV*

> d) *Romans 8:30 Moreover whom He predestined, these He also called; whom He called, these He also justified; and whom He justified, these He also glorified. NKJV*

> e) *Ephesians 2:10 For we are His workmanship, created in Christ Jesus for good works, which God prepared beforehand that we should walk in them. NKJV*

7) We are VERY purposed people! God has a plan for your life. It is our responsibility to live the plan of God for our lives.

b. We will be judged according to the fulfillment of our purpose in the Kingdom of God.

c. This is not a competition, and we shouldn't think like, "I am doing more than so-and-so," because if our works are self-seeking, self-glorifying, proud, or of the wrong motives altogether, they will be burned up.

1) The toilet cleaner at the house of God can receive as much or more commendation than the preacher according to the obedience to the calling and the motives in which the service was performed.

2) We are not all the same and each person's calling is different. One person might be very public while the other might be the prayer warrior that nobody ever sees. As each person makes their calling their priority, they will be rewarded.

C. The reason for being judged in the firmament is because there are no tears in heaven.

1. *Revelation 21:4 And God will wipe away every tear from their eyes; there shall be no more death, nor sorrow, nor crying. There shall be no more pain, for the former things have passed away." NKJV*

2. By having the judgment in the firmament, God will reveal to us the things we have done and the portions of our purpose that we did not complete because we held on too tightly, or were simply disobedient to God's call and desires.

a. There will be weeping at the Judgment Seat of Christ.

b. There will be nothing to hide in the aspect of why we did what we did and our motives.

c. The things we did not accomplish will not be hidden.

D. We will also be judged for our words.

1. *Matthew 12:36-37 But I say to you that for every idle word men may speak, they will give account of it in the day of judgment. 37For by your words you will be justified, and by your words you will be condemned." NKJV*

a. What we speak and how we speak.

III. The Rewards of the Judgment Seat of Christ

    A. Name the crowns that can be awarded.

        1. The Crown Of Life - for enduring temptation - James 1:12

            a. *James 1:12 Blessed is the man who endures temptation; for when he has been approved, he will receive the crown of life which the Lord has promised to those who love Him. NKJV*

        2. The Crown Incorruptible - For being temperate in all things.

            a. *1 Corinthians 9:25 And everyone who competes for the prize is temperate in all things. Now they do it to obtain a perishable crown, but we for an imperishable crown. NKJV*

        3. The Crown Rejoicing - For evangelizing.

            a. *1 Thessalonians 2:19 For what is our hope, or joy, or crown of rejoicing? Is it not even you in the presence of our Lord Jesus Christ at His coming? NKJV*

        4. The Crown Of Righteousness - For loving His return.

            a. *2 Timothy 4:8 Finally, there is laid up for me the crown of righteousness, which the Lord, the righteous Judge, will give to me on that Day, and not to me only but also to all who have loved His appearing. NKJV*

        5. The Crown Of Glory - For good leadership (not being lords over God's heritage).

            a. *1 Peter 5:4 And when the Chief Shepherd appears, you will receive the crown of glory that does not fade away. NKJV*

    B. We cast them at Jesus' feet to give Him all the glory.

        1. *Revelation 4:10-11 The twenty-four elders fall down before Him who sits on the throne and worship Him who lives forever and ever, and cast their crowns before the throne, saying: [11]"You are worthy, O Lord, To receive glory and honor and power; For You created all things, And by Your will they exist and were created." NKJV*

            a. The 24 Elders are the representation of the church in heaven.

IV. **Judgment of the Sinner / The Great White Throne Judgment**

A. This is totally different from that of the blood-washed saint and child of God.

    1. The Christian will not be at this judgment!

B. The only people that will be at this judgment are those who will never go to heaven. Their eternity is sealed. It will be a complete separation from God, and if a person comes to this judgment, there will be no second opportunity.

    1. *Revelation 20:11-15 Then I saw a great white throne and Him who sat on it, from whose face the earth and the heaven fled away. And there was found no place for them. 12And I saw the dead, small and great, standing before God, and books were opened. And another book was opened, which is the Book of Life. And the dead were judged according to their works, by the things which were written in the books. 13The sea gave up the dead who were in it, and Death and Hades delivered up the dead who were in them. And they were judged, each one according to his works. 14Then Death and Hades were cast into the lake of fire. This is the second death. 15And anyone not found written in the Book of Life was cast into the lake of fire. NKJV*

        a. The White Throne Judgment is the final judgment that is talked about in the Word of God.

        b. All the people from the fall of man to the finality of history to this point who were not righteous and who did not receive the blood of Jesus to wash their sins away will be at this final judgment.

            1) The holding tank of hell will be emptied for this judgment.

            2) It does not matter how powerful you were in the world.

            3) It does not matter how poor you were.

            4) It does not matter how many good things you did.

            5) It does not matter if you were sincere.

            6) The only thing that keeps you from this judgment is receiving Jesus as your personal Savior or, for those who were alive in the Old Testament, living a righteous life.

        c. There are two books.

        1) Book of Works

a) A person's entire life of works has been written in this book.

b) This is done so that people could not consider God an unjust Judge. It also shows people that they have chosen their destinies.

2) Book of Life

a) The Book of Life is where each redeemed person's name has been written.

b) When a person's name is not written, it is because they rejected the price that was paid for their salvation.

c) The people at the White Throne Judgment will not have their names written in this book and therefore will be cast into the Lake of Fire.

d. **The Second Death**

1) Hell and death will be thrown into the Lake of Fire.

a) The Lake of Fire is the ETERNAL destination of the damned.

b) Even the holding tank itself will be consumed by the Lake of Fire.

2) This final destination is one of eternal torment for Satan and his angels and all those who did not receive Christ in their hearts.

3) There will be no escape and no end to the torment.

4) Their eternal bodies will live and experience the separation and torment for all eternity, with no end!

5) My personal opinion of the greatest torment of the Lake of Fire is that you were just judged justly in the presence of the King of kings and were actually in His presence. You will know that you will never be in His presence again and that you personally chose this eternal torment. You will remember the times that someone came to you and shared Jesus, or that you had the opportunity to receive Jesus yet you rejected Him or walked away from Him. You'll go into all eternity knowing you

cannot and will not be able to have a second chance. That is the worst!!!!

Chapter 6

Tithe – Seed – Alms

Without question, this is one of the hottest topics in the church world today. The reason this is such a heated issue is because of abuse and the lack of knowledge in the body of Christ.

There is a need to bring clarity to the church with the Word of God and eliminate confusion and bring understanding for blessing. This is definitely a doctrine of the Word, designed by God Himself, so we need to understand it to be in His will.

There are three types of giving we are going to cover in this chapter. We will first deal with **tithing**, then **alms**, and finally **seed**. Each type of giving has its own principles that make up the wholeness of giving in the Bible. We will find that the very nature of our Father is revealed in giving.

Let's begin with tithing. We are going to deal with tithing from three perspectives: ***Relationship, Stewardship, and Obedience***. We will understand the fullness of God's plan for finances when we have completed this chapter.

Some say tithing was only for the Old Testament and not for the New Testament. We will show that this is not true as we continue in this chapter.

I. Tithes

    A. Relationship with God.

        1. When thinking about God and money, many never connect this with relationship and respect, but God definitely does.

            a. *Leviticus 27:30 And all the tithe of the land, whether of the seed of the land or of the fruit of the tree, is the Lord's. It is holy to the Lord. NKJV*

            b. Tithe - Strong's H4643 - *ma`aser - tithe, tenth part*
http://www.blueletterbible.org/lang/lexicon/lexicon.cfm?Strongs=H4643&t=KJV

            c. The tithe is holy.

                1) Holy - *Strong's Exhaustive Concordance* H6944 – *qodesh / apartness, holiness, sacredness, separateness.*
http://www.blueletterbible.org/lang/lexicon/lexicon.cfm?Strongs=H6944&t=KJV

2) There are some things that are God's and not for us to touch. They are holy to Him, separated to Him, not for us.

3) When I was a boy, my dad would buy maple walnut ice cream for himself. It was clear, this was his ice cream and his alone. We could eat any other ice cream in the freezer, but that was not to be touched (I hated maple walnut anyway). One day, somebody had some, and when he got home and went to get his ice cream, it was gone. He was extremely unhappy. Why? Because he had made it clear that it was his, and his alone. Some would say that is bad, but God thinks that way too. There are some things that are HIS, AND HIS ALONE.

2. The Garden of Eden is a great example for us to understand that some things are not to be touched.

a. *Genesis 2:8-9 The Lord God planted a garden eastward in Eden, and there He put the man whom He had formed. ⁹ And out of the ground the Lord God made every tree grow that is pleasant to the sight and good for food. The tree of life was also in the midst of the garden, and the **tree of the knowledge of good and evil**. NKJV*

b. *Genesis 2:16-17 And the Lord God commanded the man, saying, "Of every tree of the garden you may freely eat; ¹⁷ **but of the tree of the knowledge of good and evil you shall not eat**, for in the day that you eat of it you shall surely die." NKJV*

1) Why could they not eat of that tree?

a) Was it poison?

b) Would they understand the difference between right and wrong if they ate the fruit?

c) Why not that tree?

2) One reason was for free will. If they had no choice, they would never love God with free will because there would have been no option to sin.

3) The main reason was BECAUSE it was God's tree!

a) He separated this tree from them to partake of.

b) It was not to be enjoyed because it was not theirs to enjoy. God separated it.

4) I used to think that the reason they could not eat was that they would know good from evil, but they already had that consciousness or He would not have told them no. They would not have known right from wrong, but they did know. So the issue was not that they would finally understand right from wrong. The issue was God said for them not to eat of this tree. It was separated!

5) The results of eating this tree were devastating.

a) The consequence was that God could no longer walk with them in the cool of the day (Genesis 3:8).

b) RELATIONSHIP WAS BROKEN!

c) Touching the holy things of God interferes with our intimacy with our Father.

3. We see the relationship severance in the book of Malachi too.

a. *Malachi 3:7-8 "For I am the Lord, I do not change; Therefore you are not consumed, O sons of Jacob.* [7] *Yet from the days of your fathers* **You have gone away from My ordinances** *And have not kept them.* **Return to Me, and I will return to you,"** *Says the Lord of hosts. "But you said,* **'In what way shall we return?'** *NKJV*

1) God told His children that they were no longer keeping His principles and that was not pleasing to Him.

2) The main reason for God's reaction is because it affected His relationship with His people.

3) "RETURN TO ME, AND I WILL RETURN TO YOU."

4) When the children of God did not keep His principles, it created a separation between them and the Father.

5) His counsel was for them to RETURN TO HIM, and His response was that He would return to them.

6) WHAT WAS THE PRINCIPLE THAT CAUSED A RELATIONSHIP BREACH?

b. Malachi 3:8-10 *"Will a man rob God? Yet you have robbed Me! But you say, 'In what way have we robbed You?' In tithes and offerings.* ⁹ *You are cursed with a curse, For you have robbed Me, Even this whole nation.* ¹⁰ *Bring all the tithes into the storehouse, That there may be food in My house, And try Me now in this," Says the Lord of hosts, "If I will not open for you the windows of heaven And pour out for you such blessing That there will not be room enough to receive it." NKJV*

1) The Father is saying very clearly that when a person does not tithe or give an offering, it does not allow the relationship to be as close as it should be.

2) In our relationships there are certain things that are expected. When a person doesn't meet those expectations, or acts in the opposite way, it is hurtful and disrespectful. It doesn't stop love, but it creates strain and a gap. It stops another level of closeness until the behavior is changed.

c. Tithing is HOLY, and when we choose to willfully disobey our King, then as much as He loves us, there is a breach because of disrespect. IT AFFECTS OUR RELATIONSHIP WITH GOD!

II. Stewardship

A. What is stewardship?

B. *The careful and responsible management of something entrusted to one's care.* http://www.merriam-webster.com/dictionary/stewardship

1. *Psalm 24:1 The earth is the Lord's, and all its fullness, The world and those who dwell therein. NKJV*

2. Everything we have is not ours, but God's.

3. We are being entrusted to manage His assets while we are here on this earth.

4. *Luke 16:1-2 He also said to His disciples: "There was a certain rich man who had a steward, and an accusation was brought to him that this man was wasting his goods.* ² *So he called him and said to him, 'What is this I hear about you? Give an account of your stewardship, for you can no longer be steward.' NKJV*

5. *Luke 16:10-11 He who is faithful in what is least is faithful also in much; and he who is unjust in what is least is unjust also in much.* ¹¹ *Therefore if you have*

not been faithful in the unrighteous mammon, who will commit to your trust the true riches? NKJV

     a. The word *mammon* means money.

     b. We are called to be good stewards of God's finances.

     c. He has asked us to tithe 10%, and we get the blessing of using the 90% as we wish as good stewards.

     d. God will bless the 90% when we are faithful as His stewards to tithe the 10%.

     e. I would rather work with 90% blessed than 100% cursed.

     f. This is also a test of trust.

          1) Verse 11 says that if we can be faithful with money, which is temporary, He then can trust us with true riches which are eternal.

III. Obedience

A. Simply stated, God the King tells us to tithe.

     1. *Leviticus 27:30 And all the tithe of the land, whether of the seed of the land or of the fruit of the tree, is the Lord's. It is holy to the Lord. NKJV*

B. There are many times that it has gotten tight with our family and hard decisions have to be made with the finances. But without question, not because it makes sense, but out of sheer obedience, we have paid our tithes first.

C. When we have obeyed God in the tithe, it is now His responsibility to rebuke the devourer.

     1. *Malachi 3:11-12 "And I will rebuke the devourer for your sakes, So that he will not destroy the fruit of your ground, Nor shall the vine fail to bear fruit for you in the field," Says the Lord of hosts; 12 "And all nations will call you blessed, For you will be a delightful land," Says the Lord of hosts. NKJV*

     2. God will step in because of our obedience and rebuke the enemy for stealing His finances. Remember, the money is all God's, we are stewards of His finances.

3. We are managers of God's finances, which takes a massive load off our shoulders.

D. I explain it this way when it comes to tithing.

1. Let's say I made you a hot, steaming apple crisp pie in my glass pie dish and gave you the pie but asked for the dish back. I told you that if you gave me the dish back, I will make you another pie in the near future. You take that pie home and throw some vanilla ice cream on it and eat every portion of it. I am excited that you enjoyed it! I love blessing you with a pie that will make you happy. There is one thing though, you kept my pie dish. WHOSE TURN IS IT TO MAKE THE PIE?

a. It is your turn to make the pie because you kept the dish!

2. What does this have to do with tithing?

a. When God has blessed us with the jobs, the capabilities, and the skill sets to do a job, and we bring home the money from that job or company to enjoy. God is excited that you are being blessed and using the gifts He blessed you with to prosper. He explained in His Word that we are to tithe 10% of the increase (gross), that is the pie dish. If we eat all the pie (use all the money) and keep the dish (keep the tithe), WHOSE TURN IS IT TO MAKE THE PIE?

b. If we are not tithing, we are not positioned to have God be the Lord (the baker) over our finances. We are our own god over our own money. So when you need more, or run into a situation where you want another pie or an extra piece, it is your responsibility to make your own money. God has stepped back.

c. Give Him back the pie dish and watch Him work on your behalf in the finances of your home and business.

E. There is a heresy being taught that tithing is not for the New Testament saint.

F. The first thing I would like to address is that 99 out of 100 times, the people that claim this do not even give close to 10%. This is their excuse to not give into the Kingdom of God or live in obedience to God's Word.

1. The concept of the New Testament is MORE than the Old Covenant, not less!

2. Ten percent would be the lowest a true New Testament believer should EVER give.

3. *Acts 2:45 ...and sold their possessions and goods, and divided them among all, as anyone had need. NKJV*

4. *Acts 4:34-35 Nor was there anyone among them who lacked; for all who were possessors of lands or houses sold them, and brought the proceeds of the things that were sold, ³⁵ and laid them at the apostles' feet; and they distributed to each as anyone had need. NKJV*

5. If you are claiming to not tithe because it is Old Testament, yet give less than your all, you are not walking in the New Testament either. This usually comes down to you not trusting God with your finances, or simply, you do not want to obey God.

G. Tithing began before the law.

1. It all began 400 years before the law was established.

2. The first 10% was given from Abram to Melchizedek.

a. *Genesis 14:18-20 Then Melchizedek king of Salem brought out bread and wine; he was the priest of God Most High. ¹⁹ And he blessed him and said: "Blessed be Abram of God Most High, Possessor of heaven and earth; ²⁰ And blessed be God Most High, Who has delivered your enemies into your hand." And he gave him a tithe of all. NKJV*

3. We see that the tithe continued as a principle through the Patriarchs.

a. *Genesis 28:20-22 Then Jacob made a vow, saying, "If God will be with me, and keep me in this way that I am going, and give me bread to eat and clothing to put on, ²¹ so that I come back to my father's house in peace, then the Lord shall be my God. ²² And this stone which I have set as a pillar shall be God's house, and of all that You give me I will surely give a tenth to You." NKJV*

4. When the law came into effect, we see God confirming the principle.

a. *Leviticus 27:30 And all the tithe of the land, whether of the seed of the land or of the fruit of the tree, is the Lord's. It is holy to the Lord. NKJV*

H. Tithing was before the law, then became a part of the law. Sadly, it shows a heart issue.

1. When men tithed before the law, there was no demand because they recognized their need and the blessing of God.

2. The law made it a command because the heart of man disavowed God as their Source.

I. Is it for the New Testament?

1. Melchizedek was the high priest to whom Abram gave the first tithe.

2. He had no beginning or ending as a high priest.

3. He is a type of Christ!

4. Jesus is our High Priest from the order of Melchizedek.

    a. What did Melchizedek do? He received tithes.

    b. *Hebrews 7:1-10 For this Melchizedek, king of Salem, priest of the Most High God, who met Abraham returning from the slaughter of the kings and blessed him, 2 to whom also **Abraham gave a tenth part of all**, first being translated "king of righteousness," and then also king of Salem, meaning "king of peace," 3 without father, without mother, without genealogy, having neither beginning of days nor end of life, **but made like the Son of God, remains a priest continually**. 4 Now consider how great this man was, to whom even the patriarch Abraham gave a tenth of the spoils. 5 And indeed those who are of the sons of Levi, who receive the priesthood, have a commandment to receive tithes from the people according to the law, that is, from their brethren, though they have come from the loins of Abraham; 6 but he whose genealogy is not derived from them received tithes from Abraham and blessed him who had the promises. 7 Now beyond all contradiction the lesser is blessed by the better. 8 **Here mortal men receive tithes, but there he receives them, of whom it is witnessed that he lives**. 9 Even Levi, who receives tithes, paid tithes through Abraham, so to speak, 10 for he was still in the loins of his father when Melchizedek met him. NKJV*

    c. *Hebrews 5:10 ...called by God as High Priest "according to the order of Melchizedek," NKJV*

    d. What does the order of Melchizedek do? They receive the tithe.

5. Tithing has not ceased in the New Testament. It has gotten back to an issue of the heart.

    a. It is holy. They are God's finances, not ours.

    b. It is received by our High Priest, Jesus Christ.

c. It is a matter of the heart.

6. For those who do not believe tithing is for the New Testament, they need to be giving well over 10% or they are just using this as an excuse to not give.

IV. ALMS

A. *Matthew 6:1-4 "Take heed that you do not do your charitable deeds before men, to be seen by them. Otherwise you have no reward from your Father in heaven.*
2 Therefore, when you do a charitable deed, do not sound a trumpet before you as the hypocrites do in the synagogues and in the streets, that they may have glory from men. Assuredly, I say to you, they have their reward. 3 But when you do a charitable deed, do not let your left hand know what your right hand is doing, 4 that your charitable deed may be in secret; and your Father who sees in secret will Himself reward you openly. NKJV

1. An ALM is giving to someone in need, above your tithe.

2. <u>Greek word means - mercy, charity, a donation to the poor.</u>

3. It is giving and not expecting anything in return, and not letting people know that you have given the gift to that person or organization.

4. When giving an ALM you should not tell anyone and secretly bless someone who is struggling in their finances, food, clothing, and basic needs of life.

5. The Father says that He will reward you for giving the ALM to those in need.

   a. He might bless you with favor.

   b. He might bless you with a spiritual blessing.

   c. He might bless you with the same thing that you blessed someone else with.

   d. He will bless you as long as you do it and do not try to get your glory here on earth.

B. Who do you give alms to?

1. Giving to those in need is our responsibility in the body.

   a. *Deuteronomy 15:7-11 "If there is among you a poor man of your brethren, within any of the gates in your land which the Lord your God is giving you, you shall not harden your heart nor shut your hand from your poor brother, ⁸ but you shall open your hand wide to him and willingly lend him sufficient for his need, whatever he needs. ⁹ Beware lest there be a wicked thought in your heart, saying, 'The seventh year, the year of release, is at hand,' and your eye be evil against your poor brother and you give him nothing, and he cry out to the Lord against you, and it become sin among you. ¹⁰ You shall surely give to him, and your heart should not be grieved when you give to him, because for this thing the Lord your God will bless you in all your works and in all to which you put your hand. ¹¹ For the poor will never cease from the land; therefore I command you, saying, 'You shall open your hand wide to your brother, to your poor and your needy, in your land.' NKJV*

b. *Matthew 25:34-40 Then the King will say to those on His right hand, 'Come, you blessed of My Father, inherit the kingdom prepared for you from the foundation of the world: ³⁵ for I was hungry and you gave Me food; I was thirsty and you gave Me drink; I was a stranger and you took Me in; ³⁶ I was naked and you clothed Me; I was sick and you visited Me; I was in prison and you came to Me.' ³⁷ "Then the righteous will answer Him, saying, 'Lord, when did we see You hungry and feed You, or thirsty and give You drink? ³⁸ When did we see You a stranger and take You in, or naked and clothe You? ³⁹ Or when did we see You sick, or in prison, and come to You?' ⁴⁰ And the King will answer and say to them, 'Assuredly, I say to you, inasmuch as you did it to one of the least of these My brethren, you did it to Me.' NKJV*

c. *James 2:15-17 If a brother or sister is naked and destitute of daily food, ¹⁶ and one of you says to them, "Depart in peace, be warmed and filled," but you do not give them the things which are needed for the body, what does it profit? ¹⁷ Thus also faith by itself, if it does not have works, is dead. NKJV*

2. Blessing others is the character and nature of God Himself.

a. *1 John 3:17 But whoever has this world's goods, and sees his brother in need, and shuts up his heart from him, how does the love of God abide in him? NKJV*

3. Blessing others pleases God.

a. *Acts 10:4 And when he observed him, he was afraid, and said, "What is it, lord?" So he said to him, "Your prayers and your alms have come up for a memorial before God. NKJV*

b. *Acts 10:31 ...and said, 'Cornelius, your prayer has been heard, and your alms are remembered in the sight of God. NKJV*

V. SEEDTIME AND HARVEST FINANCIALLY

A. *Genesis 1:12* And the earth brought forth grass, the herb *that* yields seed according to its kind, and the tree *that* yields fruit, **whose seed *is* in itself according to its kind.** And God saw that *it was* good.

B. LIFE IS IN THE SEED.

1. When God created the earth, He planned to create it so that it would reproduce itself through the seed.

2. Can you imagine if the Father did not create the earth this way? Every spring we would have to go out to our lawn and wait for the Father to say, "GRASS" or the earth would be all brown.

3. Father had a plan when He created the earth to create the SEED so it would reproduce itself of the same kind, and that each kind would have the SEED INSIDE ITSELF.

4. So the life for every living creature and as we will see, other types of life and abundance are directed from the seed that is in itself.

C. So if you and I want to see ABUNDANCE in our lives, we must understand the principle of SEEDTIME AND HARVEST.

1. God the Father has not only created this principle, but he LIVES this principle. He created a LAW in this world and now lives by that law of SEEDTIME and HARVEST.

a. The Kingdom of God is likened to a seed. *Mark 4:26-29 And He said, "**The kingdom of God is as** if a man should scatter **seed** on the ground, and should sleep by night and rise by day, and the seed should sprout and grow, he himself does not know how. For the earth yields crops by itself: first the blade, then the head, after that the full grain in the head. But when the grain ripens, immediately he puts in the sickle, **because the harvest has come."** NKJV*

2. WHAT IS CONSIDERED SEED IN THE WORD?

3. The Lord made a covenant with Noah that SEEDTIME AND HARVEST will not cease.

a. *Genesis 8:22 "While the earth remains, **Seedtime and harvest,** Cold and heat, Winter and summer, And day and night, **Shall not cease."** NKJV*

1) Life of the living - THE SEED IS IN ITSELF

2) Plants – corn and sunflower seeds.

3) Animals

4) People - when a baby girl is born, she has all the eggs her body will ever use, and many more, perhaps as many as 450,000 (http://www.fwhc.org/health/moon.htm)

5) The Word of God – Matthew 13 (sower and the seed)

6) The Messiah - Galatians 3:16 - God's seed to the earth to reap a HARVEST of souls.

7) Our words - *Proverbs 18:21 Death and life are in the power of the tongue, And those who love it will eat its fruit. NKJV*

8) Our actions - *Galatians 6:7-8 Do not be deceived, God is not mocked; for whatever a man sows, that he will also reap. ⁸For he who sows to his flesh will of the flesh reap corruption, but he who sows to the Spirit will of the Spirit reap everlasting life. NKJV*

9) **MONEY** - *2 Corinthians 9:6 But this I say: He who sows sparingly will also reap sparingly, and he who sows bountifully will also reap bountifully. ⁷So let each one give as he purposes in his heart, not grudgingly or of necessity; for God loves a cheerful giver. NKJV*

D. WE CONTROL OUR SEED AND HARVEST IN FINANCES

1. What is sown is what will be produced.

2. This is not in the hands of God anymore; this is in our hands!

3. What we SOW, we shall REAP in every area of life.

4. *2 Corinthians 9:6-12 But this I say: **He who sows sparingly will also reap sparingly, and he who sows bountifully will also reap bountifully.** ⁷ So let each one give as he purposes in his heart, not grudgingly or of necessity; for God loves a cheerful giver. ⁸ And God is able to make all grace abound toward you, that you, always having all sufficiency in all things, may have an abundance for every good work. ⁹ As it is written: "He has dispersed abroad, He has given to the poor; His righteousness endures forever." ¹⁰ **Now may He who supplies seed to***

*the sower, and bread for food, supply and multiply the seed you have sown and increase the fruits of your righteousness, 11 **while you are enriched in everything for all liberality,** which causes thanksgiving through us to God. 12 For the administration of this service not only supplies the needs of the saints, but also is abounding through many thanksgivings to God. NKJV*

5. Sowing is INVESTMENT into the future, whether it be LIFE or DEATH, POVERTY, or PROSPERITY.

6. *Philippians 4:15-19 And you Philippians yourselves well know that in the early days of the Gospel ministry, when I left Macedonia, no church (assembly) entered into **partnership with me and opened up [a debit and credit]** account in giving and receiving except you only. 16 For even in Thessalonica you sent [me contributions] for my needs, not only once but a second time. 17 **Not that I seek or am eager for [your] gift, but I do seek and am eager for the fruit which increases to your credit [the harvest of blessing that is accumulating to your account].** 18 But I have [your full payment] and more; I have everything I need and am amply supplied, now that I have received from Epaphroditus the gifts you sent me. [They are the] fragrant odor of an offering and sacrifice which God welcomes and in which He delights. 19 And my **God will liberally supply (fill to the full) your every need** according to His riches in glory in Christ Jesus. Amplified Bible*

7. We like to say verse 19 is for everyone, but in context, it is meant for those who are sowing into ministry. Sowing and reaping are the principles for increase and blessing.

8. When we sow, we open a credit and debit account in heaven. As was revealed in 2 Cor. 9:6, we determine whether that account will have little or much, not God.

9. God is the provider of the seed. We have the responsibility to be good stewards of the seed to bring the harvest into our lives.

10. Many blame God for many things that He has nothing to do with. What we sow we reap. Watch your seeds.

E. THE FARMER / 2 Corinthians 9:6-12

1. One thing that is really cool about God is that He shows parallels with heaven and earth.

2. The principles of sowing and reaping are eternal principles, but can be understood through the natural process He created for the earth's reproduction and increase.

3. Each year, the farmer makes a decision to plant his ground with seed to bring forth a harvest that he can use for feed, sale, and the next year's reproduction.

4. The farmer is the one who determines the size of the harvest by the amount of seed that he desires to plant.

> a. One acre of seed planted is not going to produce the same as 10 acres of seed planted.

> b. An important clarification – this is not about how much in the sense of amounts, but in a relative term.

>> 1) Mark 12:41-44 *And He looked up and saw the rich putting their gifts into the treasury, ² and He saw also a certain poor widow putting in two mites. ³ So He said, "Truly I say to you that this poor widow has put in more than all; ⁴ for all these out of their abundance have put in offerings for God, but she out of her poverty put in all the livelihood that she had." NKJV*

>> 2) To one person, a dollar is a huge sacrifice of seed, but to another, $10,000 might be less than a dollar. So amounts are not the point. It is obedience and sacrifice.

5. We determine our reaping by the size seed we plant.

> a. 2 Corinthians 9:6-7 *But this I say: He who sows **sparingly** will also reap sparingly, and he who sows **bountifully** will also reap bountifully. ⁷ **So let each one give as he purposes in his heart,** not grudgingly or of necessity; for God loves a cheerful giver. NKJV*

>> 1) You can be a cheerful giver because you know the principles and that you cannot out-give God.

6. God provides the seed to the sower.

> a. *2 Corinthians 9:10-11 Now may **He who supplies seed to the sower**, and bread for food, supply and multiply the seed you have sown and increase the fruits of your righteousness, ¹¹ while you are enriched in everything for all liberality, which causes thanksgiving through us to God. NKJV*

1) God is the one who supplies the seed so there is no stress.

2) One day when I was getting ready for church, the Holy Spirit told me to give the pastor $100. I didn't have $100, so I told Him that He would have to provide it. I walked into church and a person walked up and gave me a handshake. When I opened my hand there was a $100 check in it. I flipped it over and signed it over to the pastor. I walked up and sowed that into his life.

3) My wife and I had a special guest at the church and the Holy Spirit told him that a certain amount of people were to give $300. I usually do not like that type of offering receiving but it was God stretching my wife and me. We knew we were supposed to give. We made out the check, post-dated it, and then gave the $300 check (I do not condone giving rubber checks). My wife went home and checked our account and found that she had forgotten a deposit of $300.

4) God provides seed to the sower! We determine to hear from Him and give it instead of eating our own seed.

b. We ask God to provide perpetual seed so we can have a perpetual harvest in all seasons.

7. Plant with expectation. Like a farmer.

a. Many have said over the years that when you give to God you should NEVER expect anything in return.

b. This is correct when it comes to ALMS, but not at all the truth about SEED.

c. Can you imagine a farmer planting an entire crop and saying that it doesn't matter if he has a harvest? That would NEVER happen.

d. When a farmer plants one corn seed, they are EXPECTING a stalk of corn with 2 to 3 ears of corn on the stalk.

1) One ear of corn contains roughly 800 kernels in 16 rows. http://en.wikipedia.org/wiki/Corn_kernel

e. If the farmer plants corn, he is expecting corn in the harvest.

f. If the farmer plants peas, he is expecting peas in the harvest.

g. If the farmer plants nothing, he expects nothing in the harvest.

h. EXPECTATION IS THE BREEDING GROUND FOR MIRACLES!

8. The Farmer's Process

    a. **They know the seed.**

    b. **They choose the ground.**

    c. **They prepare the ground.**

    d. **They plant the seed.**

    e. **They oversee by protecting the seed (thieves, animals, weeds, etc.)**

    f. **They work the seed (water).**

    g. **They expect a harvest, even though time passes.**

    h. **THEY RECEIVE WHAT THEY PLANTED WITH ABUNDANCE!**

BE A SEEDER AND RECEIVE YOUR HARVEST!